MAN, MINERALS
AND MASTERS

All Illustrations in this Book are Photographs of Mental Pictures! This book reveals by demonstration and illustration that thoughts are things and their power may be expressed through certain mineral compounds, such as organic, vegetable, animal and human and second that our thoughts may be formulated into charms or mantras according to a mathematical system called Personal Numerology or Mantras. Through the use of this system, they become more potent to execute our desires.

Charles W. Littlefield

ISBN 1-56459-571-4

THE TEMPLE OF MYSTERY
(A Mental Picture)

DEDICATED

To My Wife

CHARLES W. LITTLEFIELD, M. D.

ALL ILLUSTRATIONS IN THIS BOOK ARE PHOTOGRAPHS
OF MENTAL PICTURES

Introduction

BIOGRAPHY OF AUTHOR

DR. CHARLES W. LITTLEFIELD is a physician and surgeon, a scientist, and a writer. He is a resident of Seattle, Washington, where he has made his home for many years, and where he has been and still is actively engaged in the practice of medicine.

Dr. Littlefield's ancestors came from Scotland to America. They settled in New York when that city was still known as New Amsterdam, and long before it came under British rule. Imbued by the pioneer spirit of his progenitors, the author's father followed the development of the West, and removed from New York with his family, finally settling in Minnesota. Their experiences, and the author's early youth, were those usual to the adventurous in an unsettled country; theirs was the common lot of gallant pioneers in any land.

For a time chemistry captured the young man's interest. Its fascination has remained with him throughout his life. Analysis, investigation, and research have been a consuming passion, second only to his interest in the ills of his fellow man, and their speedy correction.

After six years of study, Dr. Littlefield was admitted to the practice of medicine by the Medical Board of Examiners for the State of Arkansas. He began his practice in 1886. But he was not satisfied with his limited training, and in 1892 entered the Kansas City Homeopathic Medical College from which he graduated in 1896.

For the past twenty years Dr. Littlefield has given much time to scientific research, experiment, and investigation in the field of biology. It was in 1902 that he first succeeded in producing life forms through the use of chemical formulas. Many of his writings setting forth the results of his investigations have been published in magazines of national circulation, and in the leading newspapers of the land.

"Dr. Littlefield disclaims having created anything. He says: 'I have only discovered the beginning and the way of life, the way nature develops the living from the non-living,' which way he terms 'Archebiosis.' He does claim to have discovered the law of form, by which nature divides the vegetable and animal kingdoms into species, building 'each after its kind.' This law he defines as follows: 'In the grouping and apportionment of the elements of organic life lies the cause of organic forms.' He has proved his assertions by the production of various forms of microscopical animal life, which have been photographed. Many of his experiments and their results have since been verified and proved by other leading scientists in America and Europe.

"Some ten years ago the author published 'The Beginning and Way of Life.' Other books written by him are: 'From Mineral to Man,' 'The Mind Control of Matter,' 'The Twelve Vitalized Tissue Remedies,' and 'Harmony of Nature and Revelation.'

"For many years Dr. Littlefield has been a member of the Christian Church, also of the Masonic fraternity. He is a member in good standing of all the homeopathic medical societies, including the King County, the Washington State, and the American Homeopathic Institute. As a general practitioner he ranks high. However the orthodox may differ from his views about life, his skill as a diagnostician and physician are unquestioned, and he has the loyal support of thousands of patients who have benefited by his ministrations during the many years of his medical practice."

(From *History of Seattle*, by CLARENCE E. BAGLEY).

Purpose of the Book

THE purpose of this book is two-fold: First, to show by demonstration and illustration that thoughts are things, and their power may be expressed through certain mineral compounds, such as are known to be a part of organic nature, vegetable, animal, and human.

Second: That our thoughts may be formulated into charms or mantras according to a mathematical system herein called: Personal Numerology, or mantras. Through the use of this system they become more potent to execute our desires.

In ancient times this system was known as the Kabbalah, or Science of the Prophets.

Mr. Ainsworth R. Spofford, late Librarian of Congress, in Volume 2, Page 194, of his *Cyclopedia*, says of the Hebrew Kabbalah:

"The Hebrew Kabbalah is a mysterious kind of science or knowledge among Jewish rabbis, *claimed* to have been delivered to the ancient Jews by revelation—specifically to Moses on Sinai — and transmitted by *oral tradition*, serving for the interpretation of occult passages of scripture.

"This science çonsists chiefly in understanding the combination of certain letters, words, and numbers, which are claimed to be significant. Every letter, word, and number of the *law* is alleged to contain a *mysterious power*. The Kabbalists even pretend to foretell future events by the study of this science."

The same claim of "A Mysterious Science" once known, but long since forgotten, is made by all the great religions of the earth.

The Veda, which is the oldest known philosophy, is based upon the *claim* to have once been in possession of the "Divine Unwritten Knowledge that issues from the Self-Existent Being."

The Yoga philosophy is based upon the *claim* that by means of abstract *meditation* its devotees are *re-united* with the supreme consciousness, *thereby developing supernatural powers*. But the *method* employed is not generally known.

The Egyptians' *claim* is based upon the possession of numerous *triads* of different attributes, the third of which proceeds from the other two. But the key to the construction of the triads was long since lost.

The Christian claim is based upon the "Power of the Creative Word," which has neither been known nor used since the time of Jesus the Christ. He referred to it as follows: "Unto you is given to know the *mystery* of the kingdom of God; but unto them that are without, all things are done in Parables." (Mark 4:11.) *No church now has the mystery.*

This "Mystery Science" in all these religions consisted in a *mnemonic* (memory) form of arranging a recital of events, either past or future, *history or prophecy*, in sets of *three* under some inclusive heading, of which *Veda Yogi Pyramid Wisdom* is the *memory key.*

Moses was taught this *mystery science* in Egypt, where the writer also learned it, instead of on Sinai, as claimed by Spofford and others. It had become the sole property of the Egyptians until after the Exodus. During the 430 years of the bondage of the Israelites, beginning with Joseph in Pharaoh's court, and ending with Moses, this *mystery science*, slowly but surely passed from the Egyptians to the Israelites who took it with them from the land of the Nile to the land of Palestine—the Holy Land. There it remained in possession of the priests and prophets until the *time* of Christ, which ended with the *death* of St. John the Revelator. It is referred to by St. Paul and two other disciples as "The Oracles of God." (Rom. 3:2.) Even St. Paul did not know the key until after he "Visited—Yonder—Paradise World," of which experience he says: "I was caught away into Paradise, and heard *unspeakable* words, which it is not lawful for man to utter." (II Cor. 12:4.)

One need not know the rules of construction of mantras in order to use them effectively. Otherwise the writer could not have employed them in fixing *thought-forms* in the mineral salts for years before the *mysteries* were revealed to him during the three initiations.

Mighty	Oneness	of	Thought	Builders
1	1		9	9

The class of persons to whom this system will appeal, are those who are governed by the supreme love of truth, and the practical results to which it leads. Such neither favor nor oppose any institution, creed, or philosophy because it is old or new. They consider everything according to its own intrinsic merits irrespective of all else. They are open to conviction, but will neither receive nor reject a thing unexamined. They live in a world of individualism, confiding in the efficacy of this self-confidence to waft them to the haven of some grand system of truth based upon the things they desire to embody in their own natures, and will be universally applicable to the good of mankind individually and collectively.

Thousands of such minds are already in the field of action, and their number is daily increasing. Thousands of others naturally belong to this class among all parties, sects, and denominations throughout the land. Such are the minds which are daily asking: How can I build my own ideals into my body and brain that I and my thoughts may be one?

Through many years of experimental research of the relation between body chemistry and mental desires, the author has answered this question in a simple, direct, and practical manner that all can understand.

Foreword

THE MYSTERY

FOR many centuries there has been in the world an ancient writing about which fascinating traditions have gathered. By some it has been called: The Word, or Holy Writ, or The Book. The latter designation will be used throughout, because it differs from all other books. Inscribed upon its pages are promises of immortal life in the body. No other scriptural writing gives this assurance, save The Book. "Let him that readeth understand." (Mark 13:14. King James version.)

It has the appearance of having been written in highly pictorial language, which implies a possibility that somewhere in its pages a *key* is held, a key which will some day be revealed and prove to be the solution of the mystery underlying the promises.

Learned men have failed to solve this mystery. The conclusion has been reached by many that, after all, The Book had no particular meaning. Others have become so enraptured with some of its phases that great bodies of followers have been organized to put forward certain beliefs based upon these doctrines.

The Book has always held a peculiar fascination for me. I have long cherished an ambition to some day search for its long-hidden secret. Many great men have shared my ambition. They have earnestly tried to disclose this secret. Although they failed, they have, nevertheless, been exalted and glorified.

First of all I would write the word "Caution," yet the goal toward which I would lead is richer by far than any hidden treasure of earth. I approach the inquiry, therefore, with a freedom entirely new to my experience, for in it I feel the sympathy of the whole world. Consistently I pronounce the Scriptural benediction.

"Blessed is he who reads these words and they who hear them and keep the saying written herein, for the time is at hand."

In John 1:1, 2, 4, and 14 we read: "In the beginning was the Word, and the Word was with God, and *the Word was God.* Through It everything was made that was made, and without It not one thing was done that has been done. In It is Life and the Life is the Immortality of men. And the *Word was made flesh* and dwelt among us, and we beheld His glory."

Herein lies the great mystery: How the "Word became flesh"? This is evident from Paul's language in writing to Timothy, 3:16. "Confessedly great is the mystery of God-likeness, God manifested in the Flesh." None of the writers of The Book claimed to understand this mystery. Indeed it is sufficient to point out that had it been disclosed to them they would not have called it a mystery, for the first and leading sense of the word is "hidden," "not disclosed."

In Revelation 10:7: "But in the days of the sounding of the seventh angel, *when he may be about to sound the mystery of God* should be finished as he announced by his servants the prophets." Therefore, as late as A. D. 96, this mystery was not finished, or revealed. Furthermore, it was to be *revealed or finished just before the seventh Angel sounded his trumpet.* Again, in Revelation 11:15, we read: "And the seventh messenger sounded his trumpet, and there were great voices in heaven saying: 'The kingdoms of this world have become our Lord's and His Christ's, and He shall reign for ever and ever.'"

From these scriptures it is evident that the mystery of "how God was manifested in the flesh," is not only to precede, but is, in fact, the reason for the kingdom of the world becoming the kingdom of our Lord and His Christ.

Since this has not yet come to pass, it is obvious that the mystery has not yet been revealed to the world.

Here I am strengthened in my purpose to search out this mystery, for I am certain that it has not yet been discovered. Also my patient search of the scriptures convinces me of another fact: Some simple thing in its essence, but of enormous import in its application, is involved in this mystery, for "He hath chosen the *little things of this world* to confound the mighty and to bring to naught the wisdom of the wise." Here is a suggestion too great to be mere accident. It is the *little* things of this world—not of heaven, yet to be discovered—which are to solve the mystery.

It is not to be expected that a mystery that was not to be made known until long after The Book was written would be revealed in its pages. Only an occasional reference, so that in after years they would serve as marks of identification when the meaning should be discovered. The statements being purely prophetic, and all focused upon one thing, until that thing comes to pass. Until that time they cannot be understood.

Furthermore, since this mystery pertains wholly to the future or "New Age," when, "All things will be made new," it is evident that nothing of the old, neither Church nor State, is a part of it. "Behold, I make a New Heaven and a New Earth wherein dwelleth righteousness" . . . *right thinking*.

Preface

WHILE yet a boy, I had an experience that started me on the road that I have followed for many years.

With my brothers, I was at work cutting corn on a farm near Muncie, Indiana, then a village. Accidentally my brother cut my foot. The resulting hemorrhage threatened to end my life. The man for whom we were working, George Walburn, was reputed to use a "charm" to stop bleeding. *This he could do without going near the injured man or animal, or even seeing the wound.* Recalling this, my brother ran to the house for aid. Walburn responded, using some magic words. No sooner were they uttered than the hemorrhage ceased. *The wound did not bleed another drop.*

After my foot was washed and dressed I asked Mr. Walburn how he had performed this miracle. He told me that a man must not tell a man, nor a woman tell a woman, but that a woman could tell a man, or a man could impart the secret to a woman, without either losing the power.

This charm consisted of quoting a certain passage of scripture, with some substitutions. Since the day I learned it many years ago I have never failed to stop bleeding, however severe. I have given this "key" to many women, some of whom have performed more wonderful cures with it than I have done.

After I began practicing medicine in 1886, the frequent use of this verse in cases of accident, or operations, prompted me to make some experiments to determine what elements of the blood the *charm* acted upon in stopping bleeding.

It was already known that certain mineral salts were necessary to the clotting of blood. I began my experiments by attempting mind control of one or more of these dissolved in distilled water. First, a drop of the mineral solution was put on the glass slide of my microscope, then placed in a temperature nearly that of the human body. As the water dried away, I would repeat the verse referred to above, the mystic three times.

While doing this I would image, or mentally picture, the form of some fowl or animal as the victim of the bleeding. Finally, I succeeded in making the crystals of common table salt, which is the most abundant salt in the blood, group themselves in the form of a chicken.

Long before I succeeded, there built up from the mineral solutions a great variety of microscopic organisms in the shape of octopi, fish, and reptiles. I do not know why.

Continued experiments demonstrated that forms of different kinds could be *predetermined* by the proportion, number, and kind of salts used. Thus I discovered that *mineral composition* is the law of living forms.

This is the reason why The Book has always held a peculiar interest for me, and why I have always believed that it contains, somewhere in its pages, the secret of *physical immortality.*

Years later, while making some experiments with the twelve mineral salts of the blood, endeavoring to discover the relation between mental states and those salts that produce clotting in case of hemorrhage, a living octopus was produced. These experiments led to the discovery of the four fundamental laws of life, as set forth in my book, "The Beginning and Way of Life."

These laws may be stated as follows:

1. "A mental image" is the beginning of every created thing. With whatever functions, faculties or qualities this image may be endowed by the mind creating it, the same will be expressed by the creature.

2. This "mental image" has the power to group the twelve mineral salts normally found in organic nature, in the exact proportion necessary to build the form, and all the tissues and organs necessary to express all the functions, faculties and qualities with

which the "mind image" may be endowed. Hence *composition* becomes the *law* of form and function.

3. Evaporation of water, a process universal on sea and land, generates *a subtle magnetism* which is the vital force of plants and animals. This force saturates the mineral salts of organic nature making them susceptible to "mental control," so that any picture that the mind accepts as true in principle may be fixed in them.

Hence the laws of creation and formation as stated in the first and second chapters of Genesis are scientifically correct.

In the first chapter we read: "And God said, let us make man in our image, after our likeness . . . male and female *created* He them." In the second chapter we read: "These are the generations of the heavens and of the earth when they were *created* in the day the Lord God made the earth and the heavens, and every plant in the field *before* it was in the earth, and every herb of the field *before* it grew, for the Lord God had not caused it to rain upon the earth and there was not a man to till the ground. But there went up a *mist* from the earth, and watered the whole face of the ground. And the Lord God formed man of the dust of the ground and breathed into his nostrils the breath of life; and man became a living soul." Thus far in our travels in search of the key to the great mystery we have learned.

1. That the creation of mental images preceded all material formations, and through their potency the mineral salts were grouped for the building of life-forms.

2. That since *composition* is the law of form and function it is of necessity the *factor* that determines species. Hence composition becomes the law of "each after its kind," as taught in the first chapter of Genesis.

The recording of all of this, more than three thousand years ago, corresponding as it does with actual demonstrations, is something more than an accident. I begin to feel a little more confident, for there is no doubt that we have found the rudiments of a governing principle which we may follow down the stream of time, and which will finally become: "The river of the waters of life, clear as crystal flowing out of the throne of God."

THE MINERAL SALTS USED

The mineral salts used in these experiments are the same kind as those found, in some proportion, in every living thing, vegetable, animal, and human. They are the ash that remains after the burning of the tissues. Time, as we know it, makes no change in them. Fire cannot destroy them. They are the *immortal* part of the physical body.

ONE UNIVERSAL LAW

If one complies with a law, though it is done ignorantly, the same results are obtained as when the law is understood. All great discoveries are made this way. Phenomena are first observed, then the law discovered which controls them.

There is one universal law which controls the manifestation of all things on the three great planes of life—physical, mental and spiritual. This is the law of apportionment and grouping of elements.

PHYSICAL PLANE

It is clearly demonstrable that the grouping and apportionment of the twelve mineral salts that are found in some proportion in every living thing, follow the physical law of: "Each after its kind." This law applies with equal certainty to every blade of grass, as well as to every vegetable, animal, and human tissue and organism.

MENTAL PLANE

The same law applies with equal certainty and effect to the building of words by the use of our letters, which are the elements of language. There are twenty-six letters in the English alphabet. At present we have 500,000 words *made* by the difference of apportionment and grouping of these letters . . . and the end is not yet.

SPIRITUAL PLANE

The same law holds true in the use of our Arabic numerals: 1, 2, 3, 4, 5, 6, 7, 8, 9, 0. By varying the kind and combination of these, any number or fraction of a number, or of anything, may be expressed. This is common knowledge.

But few recognize the fact that these digits, so called, were *derived* in prehistoric time by counting five fingers on each hand; hence the name *digit*. Nor is it generally known that the first use made of these digits, so far as we have any record, was in building the Great Pyramid of Gizeh.

The name P-Y-R-A-M-I-D means: "The division of ten," or 5 plus 5, like the fingers on our hands or the toes on our feet.

Nor is it known, except by the Old Masters, that this colossal monument, the greatest of the world's seven wonders, by reason of the number of its divisions, embodies within its structure The Principle of the mind's mastery over matter—at once the oldest and the newest occult science ever taught to mankind.

Thus, any combination of letters or words, or any two or three of which agree in *like* number becomes a "Pyramid Mantra" (Magical Formula), which, meaning when meditated upon, "according to Yoga, incarnates its occult meaning in the mineral salts of organic life as mental pictures." The constructing of these mantras was, and is yet, held as a *sacred mystery* by the Masters. Especially is this true of "Yoga Meditation," by which supernatural powers are developed.

This is a very brief outline of the results of forty years of research in a *region* which lies beyond the range of ordinary seeing or hearing. Here, in the *border land,* where mind and matter meet and blend in that union we call life, is the place which in this book is called "The Plane of Universal Consciousness."

Here I have watched matter, the obedient servant of mind, build my thoughts into material forms with an infinite exactness that must be due to some marvelous *law* we cannot understand.

I have also seen, through my microscope, answers formulated to questions that no intelligence of earth, in the present age, could possibly give. That these answers come from those who lived on earth in prehistoric times, there can be no doubt.

Most of the ancient occult science which has thus far been revealed, has never been written.

In fact it originated in the antediluvian age (before the Flood), when men walked with God, and were taught by Him. (Genesis 5:22.)

At that time there was no written language, but a mnemonic (memory) literature, which was the only means of transmitting knowledge.

Thus the whole earth remained of one language and of one speech up to the time of the *confounding* of language at the Tower of Babel. (Genesis 11:7.)

Now, it cannot be otherwise than natural that those people should have retained *in their memory* the things they had been taught. And although unable to express them in their former tongue, they would nevertheless attempt to give expression to them in a *new tongue*.

Thus it came about that particular things that suited best their new methods of thought should assume the most prominent place in their lives, and become the dominant factors in the development of a new religion.

The reuniting of these various occult doctrines, which characterize the four great religions of the earth, has been the underlying *motive* of all the communications, either in letters, symbols, or numbers that I have received as mental pictures.

Your obedient servant,

CHARLES W. LITTLEFIELD, M. D.

CONTENTS

ILLUSTRATIONS

ILLUSTRATIONS—(Continued)

Chapter I

SCHOOL OF THE MAGI

ORIGINALLY founded to teach the laws of the creation and formation of living things, the school of the Magi also taught the application of the principles involved in the advancement and prolongation of human life. Its doctrine was known as "Mazdainism," a
name derived from the supreme God Ahura-Mazda, meaning "The
Giver of Light."

Zoroaster was the legendary founder of the school of the Magi,
but as a matter of fact its origin antedates all history and all tradition. The first mention of its principles is found in the book of
Genesis where the principles are expressed as a well-defined dualism:
1. As Creation and Formation. 2. As the "Fall" wherein Good and
Evil were involved. This classification has undergone no change
or modification in historic time. "Good" has always been associated with Creative Consciousness or God. "Evil" has ever found its
origin in the physical senses.

According to the teaching of the Masters the *fall* consisted in
man's ceasing to depend on his Soul-Consciousness for guidance,
but instead, relying upon his five physical senses.

Apart from the ever-occurring actuality of this *dualism* in the life
of every man and every nation, there is recognized by the Masters
a *desire* in every man and every nation to return to the time when
the *inner consciousness* instead of the outer physical senses will
again control life. This they believe and teach to be the true spiritual ideal of every individual. They teach that this ideal was per-
sonified by the Christ; and in proportion to its development among
the nations of the earth they will all become his kingdoms. They
offer for this return from the dualism of "good and evil" to that
of "creation and formation," the conscious control of the body and

[1]

the prolongation of physical life to any desired length of time. They recognize that in the drama of life there are two persons only, the individual and his Creator.

With this realization one becomes a Magus in every sense of the term. Such a one becomes an individual without fear and without desires; dominated by no falsehood, sharing no error, loving without illusion, suffering without impatience, reposing in the quietude of eternal Oneness with God.

A Magus cannot be ignorant, for he needs only to ask and knowledge is given him. While he leans on religion he is not weighed down thereby. He knows what it is; that it is necessary to man's eternal welfare. He is never in want, for the plentitude of nature supplies his every need. He welcomes pleasure, accepts wealth, deserves honor, but is never the slave of any of them. He knows how to be poor; how to abstain; how to suffer, and he endures oblivion willingly because he is *lord* of his own happiness, and expects and fears nothing.

The true disciple can love without being beloved; he can create imperishable treasures, and exalt himself above the level of the delights that worldly honors bestow. He possesses that which he seeks. He regrets nothing that must end, but remembers with satisfaction that he has met only good in it all.

Knowing that good is eternal and evil only a deception, the Magus enjoys solitude, but he does not shun the society of man. He is a child with children, joyous with the young, staid with the old, happy with the wise. He smiles with those who smile, and mourns with all who weep. He has himself no need to pardon, for he never thinks himself offended. He pities those who misconceive him and seeks an opportunity to serve them. He knows that the only way to help others is by giving them the occasion for doing good.

[2]

The Book, as we have it today, is the traditional record of the knowledge of the mysteries of creation handed down to us from the Magi. The Christian religion recognizes and venerates the three Wise Men who came from the East, guided by a star, to adore the Saviour of the world in His cradle.

Tradition still adorns these Magi with the title of Kings, because the science of government they teach constitutes a veritable royalty of every family. This great art of the Magi is termed by all adepts the Royal Art, or the Holy Kingdom. The guiding star is that same blazing star which is the symbol in all initiations.

It is significant that this symbol is always a five-point star, emblematic of the five senses of man and their use in his pursuit of life, liberty, and happiness.

This star is now held in the beak of a Great Eagle. It will be shown that the study of this pentagram led the Magi to seek in the United States of America for one who would demonstrate their ancient doctrine of dualism in creation in life.

There exists a rigorous *formula* and five *principles* in nature which are the keys to all formation, all manifestation, and all expression on the material plane. The formula is this: In the proportion and grouping of the material elements which constitute a thing lies the cause of its form, its quality, and its functions. The comprehension of this formula is the key to all science: chemistry, language, mathematics—life.

The five principles are: light, sound, flavor, odor, and feeling. By the action of these upon matter all the organs necessary to put an organism in communication with its material environment are developed. Each organ, therefore, has a chemical composition and a form built especially to receive the vibrations of that principle which fashioned it.

These principles and this formula constitute the *facts* of dualism in nature. Whatsoever is has its being in unity regarded as the

[3]

beginning. Thus the great and indivisible dualism of the Masters presents itself to the mind as spiritual and material, hidden and manifest. That which *is* uses material to build an organ through which it can be made manifest.

This universal law of the indivisible and the unknowable manifesting through the knowable and the visible applies to every living thing from the amoeba to man, from the earth to the universe. Thus as St. Paul says: "For the invisible things of him from the creation of the world are clearly seen, being understood by the things that are made . . . " Rom. 1:20. Here it may be remarked that this doctrine of dualism, of creation and formation, of good and evil, which not only gave rise to, but a necessity for, the school of the Magi, needs no historic basis to support it. The proof is an ever-present reality.

Nor is there any ancient historical proof needed that the five eternal principles—consciousness, time, space, life, and mind—also write the record, in matter, of their reality. They are ever present, and the five physical senses makes man subject to them. Whereas before the "fall" they were the servants of man. Herein lies the world's necessity for the Christ. "Before Abraham was I am" was his declaration concerning his contemporary existence with historic *time*. "And the Word was made flesh, and dwelt among us, and we beheld his glory, the glory as of the only begotten of the Father," is St. John's testimony to his prehistoric life. "I am with you *always* even unto the end of the world," is the expression of his own assurance that time was his servant. None other than he has ever presumed to assure the world: "In me ye have eternal life. If ye abide in me and my words abide in you, ye shall ask what ye will and it shall be done unto you."

Being in actual possession of continued existence he also declared: "I have power (over my life) to lay it down, and I have power to take it up again." In the consciousness of this conviction he offered his own life as proof to the world that his conscious existence was not the life he lived in the physical body; that it was a thing altogether apart, above and beyond the life of the five senses.

Did he, as a prior existing conscious being, take upon himself the form of a man, from the body of the Virgin Mary, as Adam did from her prototype, the virgin earth; neither having an earthly father? The writer has demonstrated both to be a scientific possibility.

Did He then after leaving His earthly body three days and three nights in the tomb, enter it again and take it away with Him from this earth, as all Adam's descendants are promised by Him that they shall do? This, by the Masters, is frequently demonstrated to be a scientific possibility.

The affirmative answer to these questions does not transcend that which He promised: "The works that I do shall ye do also; and greater works than these shall ye do; because I go unto the Father." Here again we have a dualism which involves the fundamental items of Christian faith—the new birth and the resurrection—and when all of this has been admitted by the Church, Protestant and Catholic alike, what of the attitude towards those seeking to demonstrate the *reality* of the Christ as a Divine and operating word ever present as He promised He would be?

This question is answered for each individual by the seven words of thunder which the writer heard reverberate through the subterranean passage of the Great Pyramid at the beginning of the third initiation.

These words are the same which St. Paul heard when caught away to the third heaven. He declared them to be unspeakable. So they are. They are also the same that were sounded by the voices of the seven thunders which St. John desired to write; but he was not permitted to do so. They constitute the Seal of the 144,000 that were seen by him standing on Mount Zion, and about whom a great multitude had gathered which no man could number. They are that new name written in the *white stone* which no man knoweth but he that receives it. It may, however, be a *black stone* made so by the kisses of unclean lips, like that in the wall of the Kaaba built by Abraham at Mecca in Arabia.

These words describe a process that is going on in the life of every professed Christian whether he be Protestant or Catholic. They involve that inner consciousness "which no man knows save himself"; therefore they are unspeakable. In proof of this, hear the words: *"Thou Are Being Weighed in the Balance!"* Then read what St. Paul says: II Cor. 12:2-5; then of the name in the *white stone*, Rev. 2:17; of the voices of the seven thunders, Rev. 10:2-3; of the sealing of the 144,000, Rev. 7 and 14.

In these seven words is contained all that is certain, infallible, and eternal in religion. They provide the human mind with its own instrument of certitude as exact as mathematics, consequently each one can know for himself, and for no other, whether he is or is not at one with the Absolute. To know this, and adopt it as the rule of conduct—of life—is to endow the mind with sovereign power. This is Mastership. It is at once Hindu, Chaldean, Persian, Egyptian, Hebrew, Greek, Christian, and constitutes the controlling doctrine of the ages to come.

Long vanished from view, the School of the Magi has been replaced by semblances, mechanical merely and void of vitality. For a lack both of the knowledge of the materials used and their application to the awakening of the inner consciousness, few if any perfect specimens of humanity have been produced since the beginning of the Christian era. Nevertheless the true order still survives, though dwindled in numbers and no longer having organization. As a people scattered abroad throughout the world, they are once more to have a roll-call on earth.

Once known and supremely honored by the titles of Magi, Wise Men, Kings of the East, and Sons of God, they are now misknown and condemned under the designation of Mystics. Yet, while unknown for the most part, even to each other, their ancient vocation—that of supporting the claims of their Divine founder and Supreme Master, Jesus the Christ, each according to the gift of the Holy Spirit—they pursue, amidst a civilization which has become wholly materialistic, the one and supreme object: the personal achievement of that which will add proof to the certainty of the Master's claims.

Of all earthly orders, this, by reason of its antiquity, its universality among the nations, its object, and its achievements, is incomparably the most notable, seeing that from it have proceeded all the world's true sages, seers, prophets, and therefore all divine revelation. Its doctrine is that *one* true doctrine of existence, and therefore, of religion: The conscious oneness with God by which matter was in the beginning, and is to be again, the servant of the soul of man.

This supreme attainment was first manifested in the creation and formation of living things; then by Moses when he received the ten commandments graven on tables of stone; then by the author, according to the gift of the spirit, to demonstrate the manifestation of the Christ in the flesh. This is and was the mystery of the first creation, as it is that of the new Creation, and it must, it is confidently believed, be restored to all mankind, by which the world will be recovered from the age-long degradation of the "fall."

We have next to identify the persons represented in the gospels as fulfilling at the nativity the important function of recognition of the infant Saviour, as the same three Masters who presided at the *three* initiations of the writer, which they claimed to be. In

[7]

this identification will be found a forecast of the world's imminent future spiritual state.

If the writer's experience of the initiations be regarded only as vivid dreams, then they are as authentic from a scriptural standpoint as though they had been given during astral journeys, which, to his consciousness they seemed to be. The visions of the ancients, according to Moses, were nearly always dreams: "And he said: Hear now my words: If there be a prophet among you, I the Lord will make myself known unto him in a vision, and will speak unto him in a dream." Numbers, 12:6. "In a dream, in a vision of the night, when deep sleep falleth upon man, in slumberings upon the bed; then he openeth the ears of men and sealeth their instruction." Job 33:15.

But the initiations were not dreams. The writer had unconsciously given himself years of preparation for them. The marks of the true prophet or seer, according to the Old Testament were: 1. Their prophesies *must* agree with the doctrine of Moses and the patriarchs. 2. Only when a new covenant was to be made or a special reformation undertaken was a new prophet raised up. 3. The preparation for their work and the visions of the work always corresponded with the things to be accomplished. 4. All true prophets receive an extraordinary call from God and are always aided in their work by the Holy Spirit.

If we accept these characteristics from which to form our conclusions, it will not be difficult to distinguish a close similarity between the results of the writer's research work and the doctrine of *creation* and *formation* of living things as recorded by Moses in the first and second chapters of Genesis. Nor will it require any special effort to see in the three initiations that a world-wide harmony of all religions is the thing to be accomplished. Furthermore, since the one law, "Each after its kind," is equally applicable to the three planes of life—physical, mental, and spiritual—

it is likewise applicable to all peoples, nations, and tongues; for all physical, mental, and spiritual development—even to perfection —depend upon this law.

As demonstrator of the *conscious control of matter*—the principle of the old creation, employed in the miraculous conception of the Virgin Mary, which was the beginning of the new creation — the writer had, from the time of the first demonstration, been the recipient of communications from the three Wise Men who visited the new-born King of the Jews in Bethlehem of Judea. That he was afterwards taken on the three astral journeys into Tibet, Hindustan, and Egypt, and was given the initiations to confirm in his own mind the great importance to the world of his discoveries, the things which followed fully confirm.

In all the writer's former experiments in fixing mental pictures in the mineral salts, the mental images were either those of his own creation, such as the "fowl" and the "overshot water-wheel saw-mill," or those taken from The Book, such as "the Holy Spirit in Creation" and "Mount Zion." He had not had, nor could he have had, until the initiations were given, any experience in bringing conscious impressions from the astral world back to earth and then fixing them as mental pictures in the mineral salts. Such a demonstration seemed, to the Masters, to be essential to the completion of their plans for the harmonizing of the world's religions.

In all Oriental religions the central idea is "Soul Consciousness,' but Occidental religion is based largely upon physical phenomena: The Lord's supper, baptism, and public confession of faith. In the West the miracles of the Christ are of far more importance to the believer than is the consciousness of oneness with God; but it is this by which the miracles are produced. In the Orient just the reverse is true. They emphasize soul consciousness as the essential in religion. Things called "miraculous" naturally follow.

The most vivid impressions made upon the writer's consciousness by the first initiation were the men sitting in the attitude of meditation in certain select regions of the Himalaya mountains. Without any conscious effort by the writer this scene was afterwards fixed in the mineral salts, and photographed in the usual way.

The things most deeply impressed upon his consciousness of the second initiation were the amphitheatre with its expectant multitude; the laver containing the blood-like fluid; the leopard with the cobra in its jaws; the chair with the six-sided diagram on its side; and the seventh trumpet, given at the close of the ceremony. All these were subsequently fixed as mental pictures in the mineral salts, and in this physical embodiment were photographed. The seventh trumpet was the last picture obtained of this group. It was given in answer to the question: "Is the writer, in fact, the Seventh Trumpeter spoken of in Revelation 11:15, as he was declared to be during the second initiation?"

The four things that impressed the writer's consciousness most during the third ceremony were: The self-illuminating portion of the Great Pyramid of Gizeh, which, if ever built, will complete that cyclopean monument to the superconscious power of prehistoric man; the Angel in white; the tall Master about whose feet formed the triangular pools of fresh water, his twenty-four disciples in groups of three, five, seven, and nine; the fur of the prehistoric animal, and himself in the black robe with its white apron, cap, and veil in which he had been initiated.

As to the identity of the Masters who presided at the initiations of the writer being the same three Wise Men who visited the newborn Babe in Bethlehem of Judea, we have ample proof in The Book.

The Master who presided at the first initiation was Ezekiel the priest. His book, as found in the Old Testament, is the most remarkable description of the astral world ever printed in English.

The same principles, of concentric circles in rainbow colors, which he uses in his book to symbolize the creative work of the four Cherubim, he also used to illustrate the incarnation of the Word (Name), in the initiatory ceremony. In the fifth and sixth verses of the sixteenth chapter of his book is a positive declaration that he would visit the new-born King of the Jews immediately after his birth. In this chapter he also traces the history of Jerusalem from the time it was built by the descendants of Ham, the second son of Noah, to the time of its final destruction as foretold by Jesus; then on through the future to the consummation of the Christian Era. He it was who taught the writer how to use the rainbow lamp to bring himself into communication with the Astral World.

The Master who presided at the second initiation was Enoch, who, in his first incarnation as the son of Cain, the first son of Adam, lived during the long *spiritual age* of the earth which preceded the "fall." In his second incarnation he was the son of Jared, the seventh from Adam. During this period, which may be called the first *physical age* of the earth, Enoch was translated, or as The Book expresses it: "He was not, for God took him." The beginning of this age was concurrent with the beginning of the Bible chronology in 4004 B. C. We have no chronology for the first or *spiritual age.* From the nature of the things that transpired during this period, it must have been of longer duration than all the time which has followed it—probably many thousand years.

We find that St. Paul says of Enoch: "For before his translation he had this testimony, that he pleased God." Hebrews 11:5. This *witness* was that conscious Oneness with God which the Masters teach as essential to Mastership. This Oneness with the Father, by which the physical body becomes the servant of the spirit, was that which characterized Jesus the Christ. He demonstrated this to Peter, James, and John, on the mount of transfiguration; then again by the resurrection and ascension of His physical body after His crucifixion and burial.

It is not surprising, therefore, that he who had been honored as the first man to demonstrate a Mastership of spirit over matter, should be one of the Wise Men "from the East" to visit the Child who came to redeem mankind from physical death. It will be observed that the whole of the ceremony of the second initiation has to do with the destruction of this enemy of man.

The Master who presided over the ceremony at the third initiation was Melchizedek, priest of the Most High God. It is said of this priest: "Without father, without mother, without descent, having neither beginning of days, nor end of life; but made like unto the Son of God." No other man in Bible history answers to this description except the first man Adam. So Melchizedek, priest of the "Temple of On in Egypt," was, according to The Book, the incarnation—"Spirit Form"—of the first man, who, himself, had no family descent.

It is said of Christ in Hebrews 6 and 7: "Thou are a priest for ever after the order of Melchizedek." St. Paul further defines the meaning and purpose of this order: "And it is yet far more evident: for that after the similitude of Melchizedek there ariseth another priest, who is made, not after the law of carnal commandment, but after the power of an endless life. For he testifieth: Thou art a priest for ever after the Order of Melchizedek." So the order of this priesthood is that of an endless life. Priests of this order were they who came from the East to Jerusalem inquiring: "Where is he that is born King of the Jews?" Matthew 2:2.

The first initiation, presided over by Ezekiel, taught the law of the incarnation of the Word or Name—of any name.

The second initiation, presided over by Enoch, taught the law of reincarnation of the human Spirit-Form.

While the third initiation, presided over by Melchizedek, taught the return of the Spirit-Form of man.

These three eternal principles of life are the characteristics of the Christ and the basis of the world's religions.

Chapter II

THE THREE MASTERS

IN order to know the Masters, one must realize first of all that our five physical senses do not acquaint us with the truth concerning the world and the universe in which we live. It was this realization that brought the writer, more than thirty years ago, into communication with the Masters.

The Masters teach that a man's body is not his real self; that his conscious soul is his real self. No more is the physical world and the universe the real place where souls reside. Their home is in the astral world.

We all live for a time in both these worlds: During this time the majority of us live largely in the physical world, which we have a perfect right to do. A few of us learn to live in both worlds at the same time.

Jesus said: "My kingdom is not of this world," yet He invited men to live in His kingdom while they were living in the physical body. To demonstrate to mankind that this can be done, He took it upon Himself to put on the physical form of man and lived here for a time in absolute control of that form. This work He delegated to the writer. To teach mankind the conscious control, or rather, the *soul*-control of the physical body. This is the voice of the Seventh Trumpet: The Raja Yoga of the Hindu philosophy.

It is to be borne in mind that the three initiatory ceremonies were presided over by three different Masters. They will be described in the order of the ceremonies they conducted.

(* A full description of the movements of our earth and of the universe, as they were taught by the School of the Magi, will be found in the Appendix at the back of the book.)

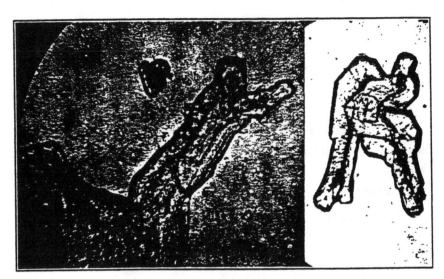

THE FIRST MASTER. Initials: "A. B."

It is interesting to note that the three Masters described in Chapter II to correspond to their initials. This law of thought builders was found to work out in all of the

$$\frac{9}{\text{mental-pictures}} \quad \frac{9}{\text{made.}}$$

FIRST MASTER

The first Master was of slender build, and not more than five feet. tall. His complexion was dark. His hair was heavy and very dark, and his beard was black. He wore a crimson turban of some soft, rich material with high lights such as satin reflects, yet it was not of that texture. The garment he wore was a black robe that fell in thick straight folds to his feet. Here again was a fabric unfamiliar to the writer, as it was soft and gleaming, yet with a heavier quality than the silk used in the robes worn by our judges.

When this Master spoke his voice was clear, yet low. His words seemed to be chosen carefully, and were enunciated with a precision which showed him to be a master of the English language.

This Master knew the history of the earth from its beginning. He knew of its preparation for the advent of life upon its surface; of the clock-like regularity with which the four principal groups came into physical existence; of the causes which produced each group; the Radiata, the Mollusca, the Articulata, and the Vertebrata, and of the law which prevented any one group or species within the group, from ever becoming like any other group or species.

The writer was amazed to learn from this Master that man came first in the order of creation. He was informed that before a plant was in the earth, or an herb grew, man was here; that he was therefore a Co-Creator with the Great Universal Consciousness; that man's body was a direct act of the Spirit Consciousness, and that all other forms of physical life are the result of man's desire to create. He called the writer's attention to the statement in The Book that: there was no plant in the earth, nor did any herb grow until after there were men to till the ground. (Gen. 2:4-5.) The departure from this state of creativeness to dependence on the five physical senses, constitutes the "fall of man."

The first Master pointed out that there "never was a time when man was not." The "beginning" spoken of in your scriptures refers to the origin of our earth and the manifestation of life upon it in physical form. All forms that were created by man were here before the fall. Since then many of the first forms have become extinct through death; and from death and decay thorns and thistles have sprung up to encumber the earth.

When the writer inquired why the earth had groped so long in darkness, the Master replied: "The great clock of time has its times of darkness and of light; its days and its nights. This is what your scriptures mean by: 'The evening and the morning were the first day.' These 'six days' were just so many revolutions of the 'hands' of the Clock in periods of 25,800 years each."

The writer then asked the Master to speak of himself. To this question he replied:

"The continent of Atlantis was the place of my last manifestation in the flesh. This was centuries before the building of the Great Pyramid. The language my people spoke was Zansar, very similar indeed to our present English. It was then a universal language, and as such had nothing in common with any modern dialect."

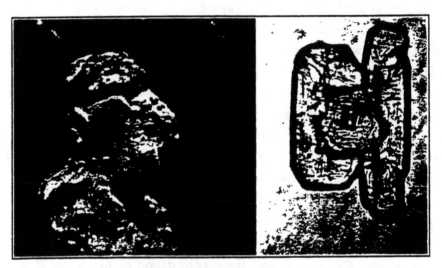

THE SECOND MASTER. Initials: "C. I."

SECOND MASTER

The Master who presided at the second initiation was of rather heavy build, blond complexion, full round face, and had brown hair. His Van Dyke beard and mustache were slightly gray. He was probably six feet tall and well proportioned. He wore a veil. Anyone might mistake him for a present-day banker, a prosperous merchant, or a captain of industry. The writer quickly discovered that he was well acquainted with the past and present methods of business men.

[18]

To the writer this second Master explained that he was born and reared on the continent of Pan, which the Pacific ocean submerged during and after the Flood. His life there antedated by many thousand years this cataclysm. During this time men lived from 600 to 900 years. It was very common, he said, to have family reunions where representatives of ten generations would be present. There were no rich; no poor. Distinction of class on the basis of worldly possessions was unknown. Men and women were equal in all rights and privileges, except that the woman was the personification of the nation.

"Our system of government," the Master continued, "was very much like that of the United States, with one marked exception: No special salaries were paid our elective officers. They served for honor's sake. The business of our Congress was to look after the welfare of the people as a whole. Our executives were concerned with seeing that each part of the country was developed equally with every other part, according to its need. The more any section of the country produced, the more they had to lend to those in need of their products. We had no such thing as money. It was the business of our judicial electives, national and local, to keep a record of these exchanges of products between different sections. Those who produced an over-supply for their locality, at the close of the season's exchanges, had no surplus. Those who did not produce enough, had no lack. Every section was supplied according to its necessities. There being no profit in this exchange of products, there was no incentive to crime. In consequence, we had no penal institutions. There being no poor, we had no need of the poor-house. The only class distinction was between the industrious and the sluggards. 'They that would not work, neither could they eat.' Such people, however, were very few indeed.

"Among other duties of our executives was that of providing prospective mothers with the necessary things to make life comfortable, and enjoyable. It was the duty of the husband to report to the proper authority as soon as the wife became *enceinte*. Immediately all that was necessary to make her soul happy and her body healthy was provided.

"The prospective mother had, by reason of her condition, become the hostess who was to entertain a guest of our nation. As such she was treated with all possible consideration. The new citizen-to-be had honored our people by choosing to become, for a time, a member of our national life. As such, from the moment of arrival, in all the many little nameless attentions it was in the power of the mother to bestow, she made it plain to the child that she deemed it her honored guest."

Reminiscently the second Master continued to picture the land in which he had lived and the manner of life there. "It was the custom to present the child on the eighth day to the authorities for registration. At this time all children of the same age would be brought by their parents before a tribunal consisting of a body of men similar in power and jurisdiction to your Supreme Court. The mother, with the child in her arms, would be seated with solemn ceremony in the chair of the Chief Magistrate. Indeed, for the moment she *was* the Chief Magistrate. She was addressed by the members of the Tribunal as: 'Your Majesty, the Queen.' To the question: 'What is your pleasure regarding your newly-arrived guest?' she replied by handing a memorandum of her plans for the baby, according to its sex, to the Chief Clerk of the Tribunal.

"Without any examination of the memorandum, while all present stood, one of the Magistrates would reply: 'It is the pleasure of your nation to carry out your Majesty's plans.'

"Does it appeal to your sense of the fitness of things," the Master inquired, "that any child born, reared, and tutored under such conditions of home life and government could be a sluggard, a criminal, or a traitor? It is unthinkable that an honored guest of a nation would violate its laws and its customs, and it is equally inconceivable that a guest in a home would do anything to wound the feelings of the hostess or in any way disturb the order of the household.

"Every child was not only a guest, together with its brothers and sisters, in its own home, but it was equally a guest among others, in the particular section of our country in which it lived. As such it took part with equal zest in all the plans of the host and hostess. Thus each section was constantly striving to exceed the others in the quality and quantity of things produced. All work was pleasurable competition. All worked to carry out the plans of her Majesty, the Queen—the Mother."

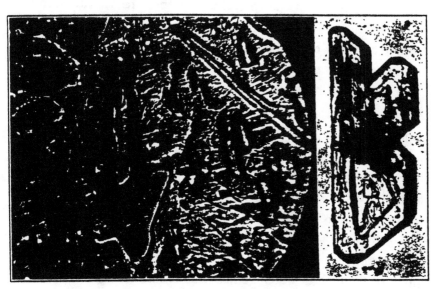

THE THIRD MASTER. Initials: "I. B."
These pictures were the result of meditating upon the appearance of each Master as the writer saw him. The initials were formed in the mineral salts in answer to the question: "What is his name?" Or "What are his initials?"

THIRD MASTER

The writer can best describe the personality and appearance of the third Master by reference to the scene where these conversations took place.

At the close of the third initiation the three Masters accompanied the writer to a distant place in the desert. Here was found, spread out upon the sand, the fur of a large prehistoric animal. The hair, or wool upon it was not unlike that of the American raccoon. The head, still attached, resembled this animal. Here the first and second Masters seated themselves, their legs crossed with the feet under the thighs, after the fashion of the desert.

The third Master stood a little distance away, probably a hundred yards. Prior to this time the writer had been treated as a pupil. Now he was made to realize, by their respectful deference to his opinion upon some matters, that he was one of them. While the other two had been speaking of themselves and the customs of their native lands, the third Master would occasionally look toward the sky as though he were expecting someone.

As the Master stood there waiting, the writer had an opportunity to study him closely. He was not less than eight feet tall, and very slender. His head was long, in harmony with his body, rather flattened from the forehead backward. The long face was topped by a high forehead, and the nose was heavy, but well shaped. His hair and beard were like fibers of fine silk, and his hands and fingers were also long and slender.

While studying this third Master the writer noticed a small triangular pool of clear water gather near where he stood. This was followed immediately by the sudden appearance of twenty-four men who stood in groups of three, five, seven, and nine. By turns these groups would pass before the Master in the order given. After they returned to their places, pools of clear, fresh water also gathered at the feet of each.

Observing my interest in this phenomena, the Master explained that these messengers were being prepared to make long journeys into the desert to give aid to those in need of help. Water being the most necessary element of life, as well as the most burdensome, only those whose names contained certain letters corresponding to the hieroglyphic symbolizing water could be endowed with this gift. Therefore, none others were permitted to go.

After these messengers had departed on their missions of mercy, the Master addressed his remarks to the writer: "Egypt is my native land," he said. "Its ancient glory has departed, but it will return. My first breath was at midnight at the time now known as the Vernal Equinox, March 21, 53,770 years B. C. It was on this date that the lines were laid upon the earth for the foundation of the Great Pyramid of Gizeh."

At this he stooped and drew on the sand with his finger a ground plan of the skies at that date. Inviting the writer to come over to the spot, the Master pointed out the position of Alcyone, the brightest star of the Pleiades in the constellation Taurus, as it stood on the meridian at midnight; and to Alpha Draconis, the Serpent in the northern sky, the pole star at that time.

He also placed in the drawing Sirius, the brightest star in the heavens, just rising in the southeast. It is estimated, he said, to have thirteen times the sun's magnitude.

"This is heaven's prophecy of the future greatness of your country, the United States of America."

Then rising and extending his right arm toward the place of this star he slowly moved his long, slender hand across the heavens from the southeast to the northwest. As he did so he quoted: "The heavens declare the glory of God; and the firmament showeth His handiwork. Day unto day uttereth speech, and night unto night sheweth knowledge. There is no speech nor language where their voice is not heard." Then he added in a meditative mood:

[23]

"But the carnal mind understandeth not the things of God, neither can it know them, for they are spiritually discerned.

"We three are those of the School of the Magi who journeyed to Jerusalem to visit the new-born King of the world. While the Babe lay in His mother's arms, we discussed our mission with her Majesty Queen Mary, and were much surprised to learn that the then ruling monarch, King Herod, had forbade the observance of our age-long custom of pledging the support of our school to the care and education of our youth born in foreign lands. So we gave of our substance that his father, Joseph, might bring the Babe to Egypt at the earliest possible time.

"It is, of course, a matter of history that 430 years before the giving of the Law to Moses at Mount Sinai, the promise of God was given to Abraham the Chaldean, that in his seed should all families of the earth be blessed.

"It is also a matter of ancient geography that Chaldea was the southern part of Babylonia, or, in a wider sense, corresponded to Babylonia itself. The name *Chaldeans* was especially applied to the Babylonian Magi. This school was devoted to the pursuit of astrology and magical science. It had its origin in the ancient continent of Pan. Masters of the school built the Great Pyramid of Gizeh.

"Abraham was born at Ur in Chaldea at midnight of the Vernal Equinox, 2170 B. C. This was the third anniversary of the building of this great monument. He migrated, accompanied by his wife Sarah and his nephew Lot, to Canaan, where he led a nomadic life for 175 years. His two sons, Isaac and Ishmael, were the progenitors of the Israelites and the Arabs. The former gave us the Hebrew and the Christian Scriptures. The latter gave us our science of numbers, upon which the recording of all facts in science depends. Both nations descended through Abraham from the School of the Magi.

[24]

"When the young King of the World arrived with his parents in Egypt, we were delighted to find him already conversant with the science of Creative Consciousness. We had long been expecting One who would reestablish the government and customs of the lost continent of Pan. We found his wisdom so far exceeded that attained by our school that we called all the Masters from the various countries of the world to hear him expound the science of divine emanations."

Chapter III

THE CUBES

IN the city of Mecca, in Arabia, near the eastern shore of the Red Sea, once known as the Arabian Gulf, there is a square edifice, thirty feet in all its dimensions, called the Kaaba, or Cube. It is the sacred shrine to which Moslems make their annual pilgrimage. At the southeast corner of the Kaaba, built into the wall, is the famous "black stone," or *Keblah,* which is devoutly kissed by all pilgrims. According to Mussulman tradition this "stone" was originally a dazzling white, and was brought from heaven by Gabriel and given to Abraham when he was erecting the Kaaba. Mohammed, a descendant of Abraham through Ishmael, the son of Hagar, the Egyptian, was born at Mecca A.D. 571. He was the reputed founder of Mohammedanism. His followers call their creed Islam, which means: "Entire submission to the decrees of God"; and the formula of their faith is: "There is no God but Allah, and Mohammed is his prophet."

The Mohammedan faith further embraces the following points: 1. Belief in God, who is without beginning or end, the sole creator and Lord of the Universe, having absolute power, knowledge, glory, and perfection. 2. Belief in his angels, who are impeccable beings, created of light. 3. Belief in *good* and *evil* genii, who are created *from smokeless fire,* and are subject to death. 4. Belief in the Holy Scriptures, which are his uncreated word revealed through the prophets. Of these there now exist, the Pentateuch, the Psalms, the Gospels; and, in incorruptible form, the Koran. 5. Belief in God's prophets and apostles, the most distinguished of whom are Adam, Noah, Abraham, Moses, Jesus, and Mohammed. 6. Belief in a general resurrection and final judgment, chiefly of a physical and not of a spiritual nature. 7. The belief, even to the extent of

[27]

fatalism in God's absolute foreknowledge and predestination of all events, both good and evil. In short, Mohammedanism includes all of the faith and far more of the duties of Christianity than is either believed in or practiced by orthodox Christians.

Ishmael (Hebrew, Yishmael, "whom God hears") was the son of Abraham and progenitor of Mohammed; born 1910 B.C. It was predicted he was to become a "great nation." He married an Egyptian wife and had twelve sons and one daughter, who became the wife of Esau the twin brother of Jacob, the two sons of Isaac, the son of Abraham by Sarah.

Esau was the eldest son of Isaac. His name signifies "hairy," and was due to his singular appearance at birth, being "red all over like a hairy garment." He was the progenitor of the Edomites, who dwelt on Mount Seir, a country known in New Testament times as Idumea, which lay to the south of Palestine. These people were first subdued by King David, a descendent of Jacob, then regained their independence to be again conquered by Amizah the eighth king of Israel, then again by Ahaz the twelfth king; and finally by Nebuchadnezzar during his invasion of Judea. Thus their identity was finally lost by intermarriage with the Persians. During their national independence their chief city Petra, meaning "stone," contained the most remarkable rock-cut temples in the world. These now lie in ruins. It has been shown the writer by mental-pictures that the modern representatives of the Edomites are the American Indians.

Jacob was the second son of Isaac and the grandson of Abraham. These were the first three Masters of the School of the Magi, and called out of Chaldea to establish a new race of people and a new government in the world. It was Jacob who was first called Israel, which means *the hero of God*. Hence the Hebrews from him were called Israelites. He, with his twelve sons, and one daughter, were finally compelled to flee into Egypt to escape starvation from a seven years famine. Some years previous his favorite son, Joseph, had been sold by his eleven brothers to some Ishmaelite merchants who carried him into Egypt. Here, through a *cipher code*—a mantra—known only to the Magi, he interpreted a dream of the reigning Pharaoh by which the king was forewarned of the approaching seven years famine. For this he was subsequently made the highest officer of the Court.

While Joseph was vice-regent of Egypt he married the daughter of Potiphera, a priest of the temple of On. Two sons were born from this union: Ephraim and Manasseh, each of whom, through the final blessing of their grandfather Jacob, became the head of a tribe. Thus from twelve sons and their families, together with their father Jacob, who went into Egypt to escape starvation, we find *thirteen* tribes, and their leader Moses, camped at Mount Sinai in Arabia, 430 years after God had promised Abraham: "In thy seed shall all the nations of the earth be blessed."

In the book of Exodus may be found the history of how God gave to Moses the Ten Commandments—ten numbers, 1, 2, 3, 4, 5, 6, 7, 8, 9, 0—afterward known as the Law, inscribed on a tablet of stone; how He appeared to Moses in a cloud on Mount Sinai and said to him: "Thus shalt thou say to the house of Jacob, and tell the children of Israel; ye have seen what I did unto the Egyptians, and how I bare you on eagle's wings and brought you to myself." This is the beginning of our national eagle emblem, and of the original thirteen colonies of the United States of America.

After giving the Law, God commanded Moses to appoint his brother Aaron, of the tribe of Levi, to the office of high-priest. which was afterward made hereditary in his family. Then he instructed them in the building of the tabernacle that was to be a sanctuary where all the sacred utensils were to be kept during their travels to the land promised to Abraham, their father, 430 years prior to this time.

This tabernacle was in the shape of a parallelogram, 45 feet long, 15 feet wide, and 15 feet high. That is, it was in length three times its width or height. The interior was divided by curtains into two compartments, the outer, the sanctuary proper, and the inner, the Holy of Holies. In the sanctuary was on the north, the table of shew-bread, on the south, the seven-pronged golden candlestick, and in the middle, near the inner curtain, the altar of incense.

In the center of the Holy of Holies stood the ark of the covenant. This contained a golden pot holding the manna, and Aaron's rod that budded, and the stone tablet of the covenant. Above, upon each end, were the cherubim of glory overshadowing the mercy seat.

The sole care of the tabernacle, its furniture and utensils, together with the costly curtains that formed the court which surrounded it, was the sacred duty of the tribe of Levi.

As Israel marched from Sinai through the forty years wandering in the wilderness, and across the Jordan into the land of promise, wherever they camped the priest would first set up the tabernacle, then the tribes in groups of three, would camp on each of the four sides in the following order: On the North: Dan, Asher, Naphtali; on the East: Judah, Issachar, Zebulun; South: Reuben, Simeon, Gad; West: Ephraim, Menasseh, Benjamin. Each group also had a camp standard which would be set up immediately after the tabernacle. On the North an Eagle; on the East a Lion; on the South a Man; on the West an Ox. These camp standards have, consciously or unconsciously, been adopted by all nations founded by the descendants of these tribes.

Near the center of the Great Pyramid of Gizeh there is a room called the King's Chamber. In the center of this room is a coffer, 144 inches long, 72 inches high, and 72 inches wide. If it were cut in two equal parts, each half would form a perfect cube of 72 inches in every direction. — 7 — 2 — 9.

The ark of the covenant in the Holy of Holies corresponds to the same rectangular shape in every particular. If it were cut in two equal parts the line which would divide them would leave a cherub on the top center of each cube.

This ark was the residence of God, and he specified his place of meeting, as: "between the cherubims." That is, on the *dividing* line. This line was not to be seen by the eye nor was it conceivable by the senses. Yet this was the meeting place of the perfect *One*.

There can be no mistake as to the likeness of these four cubes: The Holy of Holies in the tabernacle was just one-eighth the size of the king's chamber in the pyramid; and the ark in the holy of holies represented two cubes, exactly as did the coffer in the king's chamber; and the same relative proportion in size characterized their relation to each other.

When the coffer had its lid it represented a surface of seventy-two square feet. The lid on the ark of the covenant represented a surface of twelve square feet. Thus the numerical relation of the Holy of Holies to the king's chamber was *one to eight;* while that of the ark to the coffer was *one to six.* We shall have further need of these numerical values. The same relation of the size of the cherubim to the numerical standard of the plan of the Great Pyramid also identifies them both as of similar meaning. The cherubim were *ten* cubits high. It was at the exact center line between them where God talked with Moses. For every nine feet the Pyramid rose skyward, it inclined *ten* feet inward to a common center, which *center* was a prophecy of the Christ.

In the school of the Magi, the primal one, or Cube, is taken as containing all material and all life within itself. It is male-female; but when division took place, the one became two separate individuals, as *male* and *female*, each had to be a perfect one—a perfect cube. To make therefore a *perfect one,* which would combine these *opposing* entities, which yet attract each other as negative and positive, in the production of progeny, also male and female, it required just eight of the small cubes, viz.: four males and four females to make the larger family.

The king's chamber region in the Great Pyramid is the great cube of this union; and the king's chamber as to its lenegth is twenty cubits, was the eighth part of the whole cube, and was an oblong of *two cubes,* or in itself, male-female.

The division of the cherubim, first into two, one cherub on each cube; then into four by the extension of their wings to each side of the Holy of Holies until they were in contact with each other and the wall; pointing as they did, due east and west when the tabernacle was set up, they showed that the high priest, when he entered the Holy of Holies, stood beneath one wing of each cherub, representing therefore both male and female in his ministrations. God met with him on the other side, also beneath one wing of each cherub, and also blessing both male and female.

The astronomical, or better, astrological features about the setting up of the tabernacle were plain. The entrance was toward the rising sun, or the vernal equinox. The Holy of Holies was in the west end of the structure, toward the place of the setting sun, or autumnal equinox.

The great quadrangle was oriented to the four winds, or North, South, East, and West. The brazen sea, or laver, had on its ledges the ox, the lion, the man, and the eagle, which were the camp standards of the twelve tribes, by which each tribe knew its camping place about the hollow square.

Let us imagine a large circle divided into four quadrants of ninety degrees each, or three times thirty, in each quarter. There would be twelve of these 30-degree spaces. The tabernacle and the court around it was a square, and was cared for by the Levitical priesthood. The twelve tribes camped about this square in a great circle, and they thereby represented the four quadrants of the great circle of the heavens, each space of thirty degrees containing one sign of the zodiac.

The two united cubes of the coffer in the king's chamber and those of the ark of the Holy of Holies, not only represented life as a whole, male-female, but also the two special acts, creation and formation, by which life is made manifest in physical form. A cube has six sides. It is therefore the physical expression of the six days, or ages of creation, as recorded in the first chapter of Genesis. The cube representing the male is the creative principle. The one representing the female is the formative principle.

When Abraham built the Kaaba in the city of Mecca, which his descendants the Arabs born to him through Ishmael the son of Hagar, the Egyptian, afterwards used as a place of worship, he knew, as a member of the school of the Magi, that his descendants born to him through Isaac the son of Sarah the Chaldean, known as Israelites, would become slaves to the nation of the slave-girl mother of his illegitimate son.

He knew that the descendants of Isaac, in which seed all the families of the earth should be blessed, would some day return from slavery to Mount Sinai in Arabia and receive a law, and be organized as a nation under a religious ritual that would be symbolized by a cube.

Not only was the cube the symbol of the things above, as well as the symbol of things below; it was also used to disclose the things of the past as well as to predict the things of the future, both of individuals and of nations. The cube, unfolded, becomes, in superficial display a cross proper, which as a matter of history was once the symbol of shame and degradation, but is now one of glory and exultation. Symbols, like individuals and nations, once master then slave; once glory then shame.

"For it is written, that Abraham had two sons, one by the hand-maid, and one by the free-woman. Howbeit the son by the hand-maid is born after the flesh; but the son by the freewoman is born through promise. Which things contain an *allegory;* for these women are two covenants; one from Mount Sinai, bearing children unto bondage, which is Hagar. Now this Hagar is Mount Sinai in Arabia and answereth to the Jerusalem that now is: for she is in bondage with her children. But the Jerusalem that is above is free which is our mother." (Gal. 4:22-26.)

In the school of the Magi the triangle is the symbol of the male, the circle of the female. In its number code both have the value of *life* (5). "And he carried me away in the spirit to a great and high mountain, and showed me that great city the Holy Jerusalem descending out of heaven from God.

"Having the glory of God: And her light was like unto a stone most precious, even like a Jasper stone, clear as crystal.

"And had a wall great and high, and had twelve gates, and at the gates twelve messengers, and names written thereon, which are the names of the twelve tribes of Israel.

"On the east three gates; on the north three gates; on the south three gates; and on the west three gates.

"And the wall of the city had twelve foundations, and in them the names of the twelve apostles of the Lamb.

"And he that talked with me had a golden reed to measure the city, and the gates thereof, and the wall thereof.

"And the city lieth four-square, and the length is as large as the breadth, and he measured the city with the reed, twelve thousand furlongs: the length and the breadth and the heighth of it being equal." A cube. (Rev. 21:10 to 16.)

Early in 1914 while making some experiments in fixing mental-pictures in the mineral salts, the writer asked: To whom did God say: "Let *us* make man in our image and after *our* likeness?" In answer to this question an inscribed tablet was fixed in the salts. In the center of the tablet is an opening occupied by certain columns of lights and shadows which outline a human form.

When the mental-picture of the *book of mystery* was given, the key to the number code 2:6:1, shown on the outside lower edge of the left-hand cover, revealed not only the meaning of the ten triangles shown the writer by the Angel, but also of the two cubes and of the map of the United States of America: "My people united." Furthermore, this code reveals why the median line between the two cubes of the ark of the covenant was chosen as a meeting place of God with men after the "fall."

While the outer surface of the cube has six sides corresponding to the six days of creation, the seventh, or day of rest, is symbolized by the whole of its *interior*, the dwelling place of Deity.

So the two cubes, formed by the grouping of the ten triangles while meeting on a common line in the center, the *interior* of the lower one symbolizes the Consciousness of man, the upper one the Divine or creative consciousness of God. As shown by the number code: the "mind of man" meets the Creative Word on the dividing line between the two.

When Abraham built the Kaaba, ages before the birth of Mohammed, he gave to the country from which he was soon to take his departure a mark of identification of his people when they should return 430 years later. The Kaaba, therefore, became at once an object of veneration as a Pantheon of the presence of God, its interior His dwelling place. God to them, as an absolute being, having no form or name, cannot and may not be represented under any image, or by any material structure. The Kaaba represented him only as being *in* his creation and not of it.

When Jacob, the son of Isaac and grandson of Abraham, returned to his uncle Laban's home to take for himself a wife of his mother's people, the Kaaba took on, for them, a new virtue: that of rejuvenating the reproductive or creative powers. When the unexpected kinsman related how his own father Isaac had been born, after the grandfather and grandmother had both passed the generative years, the Kaaba became the shrine of this mysterious power of God as well as of his presence in the *first* creation.

THE GATE TO HOLY CITY
The "Elomata."
(See inscription over gateway.)

THE TOWER OF CREATIVE FUNCTION

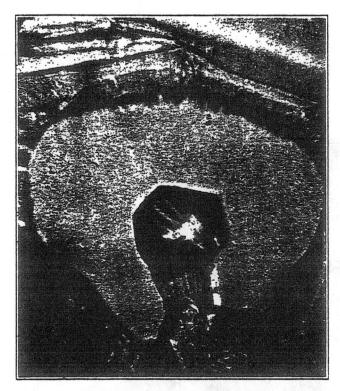

CUBE. THE SYMBOL OF MIND.
See: Table of Numerology, Page 93

38

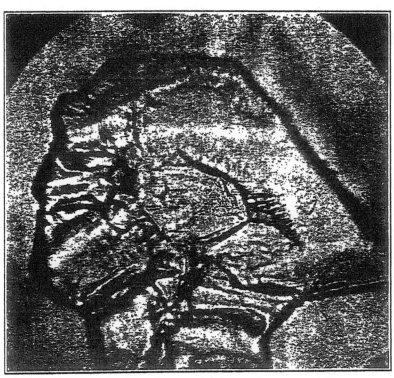

Mantra: THE HEAD   of   SPHINX   —   ORACLE
              ———   ———   ———
               9   9   9

FIRST INITIATION—Tibet

Chapter IV

STONE THRONE OF FUTURE KARMA

First Initiation—Tibet

The beginning of these three strange experiences shall be related exactly as they came to the writer in dreams. They came without premonition or warning.

Having retired at about the usual hour, the writer, as is his habit, promptly fell asleep. Presently he seemed to be following a very steep and narrow road, from which he looked down upon a small village of scattered cone-shaped dwellings. These he recognized from pictures he had seen as those used by the natives of Tibet. The writer was greatly puzzled by his surroundings and was about to ask a question of the three men who were his companions. Before he could speak, however, his thought was answered.

"You are being conducted to a monastery in the remote fastness of a mountain in Tibet," one of the men explained. "It is used as a meeting place for the Masters, and for introductory ceremonies for the candidates for initiation, into the mysteries of the "Veda Yogi Pyramid Wisdom."

While he was yet speaking we came upon a very ordinary looking cabin, seemingly hewn from, or dug into the rocks, and closed by a door that appeared to be a single slab of a large log.

The Master who was leading the way placed his hand gently on the door which opened outward as if to follow his hand, revealing within the entrance two doors which, swinging from opposite sides and meeting in the center, closed the way that had just been opened by the first door. On one of these half-doors was a white cross, while the other half had a smaller door through it which closed with a shutter. As we passed through these companion doors we came to another door exactly the shape made by the two half-doors when they were closed. This latter door had inscribed upon it, or rather built into it, a large letter "C." This letter enclosed a cross, pivoted at the top and bottom so that it could be turned side-wise allowing one to pass through the opening. Of the symbolism of these four doors we will speak more fully after we have studied the origin of alphabets from these and other hieroglyphics.

As we stood together just inside the opening made by the cross, the Master said:

"The characters which constitute the English alphabet can be traced back to the first hieroglyphics which primitive man carved upon stone, wood, and metals, to record the inherent impulses of his own nature which impelled him to action.

"These early characters were drawn because he saw in the things they represented powers and qualities similar to those he realized were within himself. Either by observation of their habits as in the case of birds and animals, or of properties and use, as in the case of inanimate things, he saw they not only possessed similar powers as those in himself, but believed they would aid him in exploits where such powers were needed. In order to avail himself of the aid of any particular thing he must prove his allegiance to it by calling himself by its name. Thus it became the custom to allow a boy to choose the name of that bird, animal, or object in which he recognized similar qualities and powers to those he desired to develop in himself.

"These are now represented, not by objects of our environment but by characters called letters, which have been substituted to make them more convenient for use. It has come about therefore, that the English alphabet is a group of representatives of the inherent motives, desires, and impulses of our earliest ancestors. To this fact, so far as the hieroglyphics are concerned any dictionary will testify. Moreover, it has been the custom until very recent times to give a name to a boy that will vibrate in harmony with that which he is to be. Through his consciousness as the body develops this name becomes "The Word Incarnate."

"The dictionary will also testify to the Oriental origin of your language, for no man would choose an eagle, a lion, a cobra, or a viper to represent his aspirations and impulses were these not objects within his environment. Several of the letters of your English alphabet can be traced back to the hieroglyphics representing these."

The above, in terms chosen by the writer, constitutes the prologue to the lesson taught him by the Master during his first initiation in a remote region of the Himalaya mountains in Tibet. While they have been enclosed with quotation marks, it is impossible to imitate the Master's manner, or his diction.

After leaving the entrance of the Cross, and following some distance along a dimly lighted corridor, the writer and his companions presently entered a very dark room where no ray of ordinary light could enter. Darkness must be very dense, indeed, if the eyes do not become accustomed to it, and finally enabled to dimly outline objects. No such explanation is possible of the phenomena by which he became aware of his surroundings, and of the persons and things in the room.

After we had entered, and while the room was still very dark, one of the three Masters began to speak in a voice such as no mortal ever possessed. His words were enunciated with a clear musical cadence unlike anything the writer had ever heard. From the moment he spoke the first word the darkness began to lessen and a soft violet glow took its place.

At first the Master addressed himself directly to the writer:

[43]

"You have been invited to the astral plane as a special envoy from the material plane, to be intrusted with a mission of transcendent importance—one, indeed, of super-excellence. Your credentials were received immediately as they were drawn. They bear the seal and signature of the Cherubim. You have already been advised of wisdom from above that will prepare you to complete certain work on the earth plane. The things you shall have indelibly impressed upon your memory during the three initiations, are a part of that Wisdom. We greet you."

As the Master continued speaking the glow passed from a soft violet through the seven colors of the rainbow until it reached the red, when suddenly the room became flooded with white light. Whenever he would pause for a moment, the light would begin to fade. But as he continued speaking, not only did all the objects in the room become visible, but the walls of the cavern, which were of stone, became transparent so that objects at a great distance could be seen distinctly, and gave the impression of coming toward us at his command. This would occur when the Master spoke of any particular thing.

In this manner the writer was enabled to see distinctly three Tibetan persons sitting in selected places in the mountains in the attitude of meditation. He was informed that, in earth measurement, it was ten miles to where they were. In appearance they also appeared very close to each other, yet in fact they were many miles apart.

In the room were three large *lotahs*, or water pots, the shape of those used in India for drinking purposes. These, however, were about ten feet in diameter at the large part of the bowl, and of about the same height. They were black in color, yet they gathered and retained for a time the vibrations of the white light. When they did this there would appear on each of them, around the circle of their greatest diameter, nine different hieroglyphic figures like those from which the English alphabet is derived. In harmony with the cadence of the Master's voice, they would glow, each in its turn, as the vibrations of his words generated the colors appropriate to the nature expressed by each character.

Beginning with the lotah nearest the Master who was speaking, the nine hieroglyphics on each bowl were as follows: An eagle, a crane, throne, hand, fret work, Indian cobra, viper, sieve, and two parallel lines. On the second lotah were: a harp, a bowl, lion, owl, water sign, heart, shutter, human knee, and a new moon. On the third lotah were: a garden, lasso, two cobras, harp, chair, tree, duck, and a circle. These are the twenty-six hieroglyphics from which all written alphabets are derived.

The writer was informed that whenever he could select by his sensations and emotions as they became excited by the glow and color of the hieroglyphics, which corresponded to the several letters of his first name, he would have passed the curtain of colors, on his journey toward the *Great Inner Temple.*

There are no words to describe the heart-searching power of such a test. As the one Master described, in his more than masterful diction, the imaginations and thoughts entertained by the human mind, which prompted it to a recurrent tendency to gratify the desires of the physical body; its opposing struggle to keep itself pure; the constant guard it is compelled to keep lest, in an unguarded moment, some voluntary act may be committed that will mar the whole life by stamping upon the memory the consciousness of a thing of shame, the other two Masters stood in silence, one watching the shifting colors from hieroglyphic to hieroglyphic; while the other, never for a moment removed his eyes from those of the writer, lest he be tempted to use them in identifying his corresponding hieroglyphics.

Slowly but surely the writer became conscious of a close affinity between himself and one of the lights on the first lotah; then of a

[45]

second and a third on the same bowl. His consciousness then shifted to a light on the second lotah, then to a second one on the same bowl. Again he was attracted to a light on the first bowl, then to one on the third lotah, and the test was finished.

Deep satisfaction was expressed on the faces of the Masters as the writer recounted, in the order given above, the several hieroglyphics and their colors which, letter by letter, spelled out his first name. These seemed to tell them, plainer than words could do the innermost desires and impulses of his soul.

Again the Master spoke. "Leaving for a few minutes the subject of the personal, relative to our visiting envoy and to this initiation, let us pause and see what may be the hidden meaning of this, the most ancient, as it is the most suggestive of traditional allegories. It has not been conferred upon a spiritual entity, who has afterward been permitted to return to his mortal body, for seventeen thousand, eight hundred and eight years. This was when Yima dedicated himself to be "King of the Golden Age" during the thirteenth Ji-van-muk-ti.

"That state will return again to the world at large when the latter shall discover and really appreciate the truths which underlie this vast problem of the relation of man's body to his inner consciousness. Then no one will even think wrongly, much less indulge in wrong doing. There lies beneath all this one eternal law of nature, one that always tends to adjust the body to the mind, the Law of Karma—of cause and effect.

"This law," the Master continued, "whether used consciously or unconsciously, predestines nothing and no one. It exists from eternity to eternity; indeed, it is eternity itself. As such, since no act can be co-equal with eternity, it itself cannot be said to act, for it is action itself. Karma creates nothing, nor does it design. It is consciousness who plans and creates *causes,* and Karmic law adjusts the effects, which adjustment is not an act, but universal harmony, tending ever to resume its original position. Karma does not seek to do anything. It is itself the thing done. It does not involve others in its decrees purposely to perplex mankind, nor does it punish or reward those who seek to unravel its mysteries. It is that which happens as the result of conscious design. Karma is, therefore, an absolute and eternal law in the world of manifestation—it is itself manifestation. Indeed, it is the ever recurring decree of the great Master: "Everyone shall be rewarded according to his works."

"When mankind shall again learn that all life is *One Life;* that its varying manifestations are due to the physical body—plant, animal, or man—through which it finds expression; that Man alone is endowed with creative consciousness; that the state of consciousness of today is the Karma of tomorrow; then and then only will he come into possession of his birthright—the Master of Cause and Effect."

As the Master ceased speaking, the white light faded into red, then from orange, yellow, green, blue, to indigo and violet and finally into utter darkness, leaving an impression on the memory of the writer that can never be effaced.

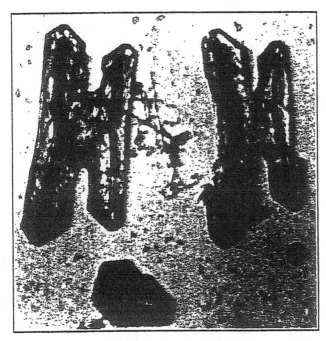

(HIGHER HIEROGLYPHICS) "H. H."

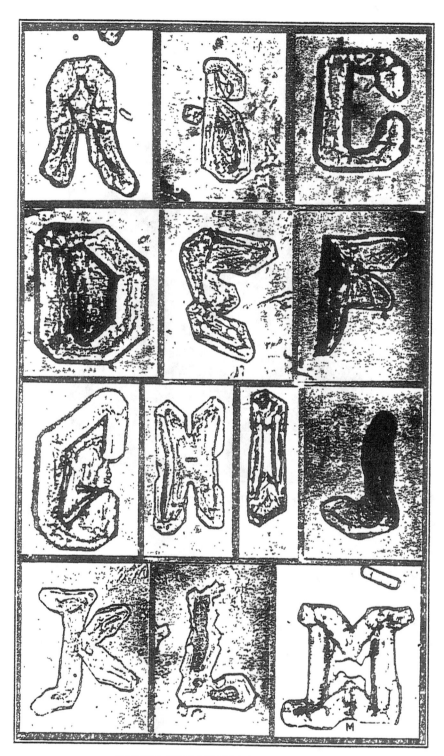

HIGHER HIEROGLYPHIC ALPHABET

50

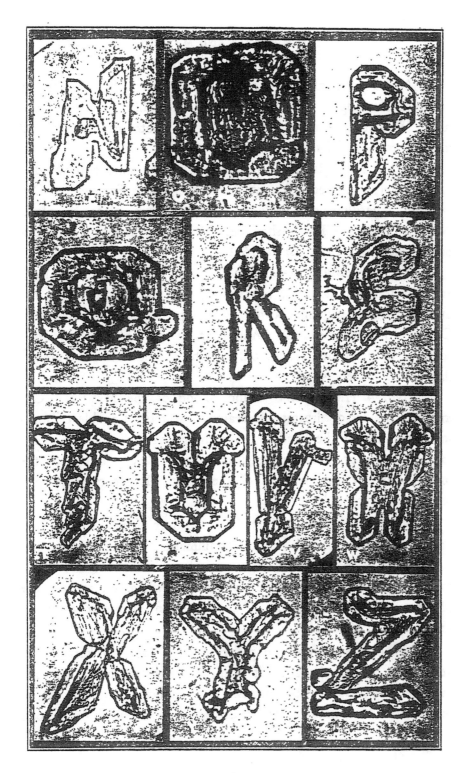

HIGHER HIEROGLYPHICS

A. No. 1 Hieroglyphic—Eagle. High ideals; thoughts mostly on spiritual things. Aspirations for an ideal life. Protective nature. Watchful. Careful. Far seeing. "Youth may be renewed like the eagle's." Psalms 103:5.

B. No. 2 Hieroglyphic—Crane. Inclined to roam and wander. Likes travel; unsettled. Always wanting change. Far seeing. Dissatisfied regardless of condition. Moves from place to place. Nothing pleases—"For it shall be, that, as a wandering bird cast out of the nest . . . " Isaiah 16:2.

C. No. 3 Hieroglyphic—Throne. Loves power. Natural leader. Sovereign in home or business. Must work alone or be the master. Wants supreme power, and to be superior in all things. Cannot work under orders. "And Pharaoh said unto Joseph: Thou shalt be over my house . . . only in the throne will I be greater than thou." Gen. 41:40.

D. No. 4 Hieroglyphic—Hand. Fond of the Mystical. Can interpret oracles or dreams. Revealer of secrets. Capable of making expert use of the hands. Loves things having a hidden meaning. Capable of direct divine illumination. "Hand is one of the most frequently used symbols of the Bible. It occurs more than one hundred times."

E. No. 5 Hieroglyphic—Fret Work. Lover of art, painting and poetry. Capable of high musical attainment. Would succeed best in painting. Capable of making practical application of knowledge to useful ends. Would succeed as overseer where a large number of persons were employed. "Tubal-cain, an instructor of every art." Gen. 4:22.

F. No. 6 Hieroglyphic—Asp, or Indian Cobra. Spiteful. Revengeful. Mean. Capable of going to any length to gain advantage of another. Also possessed of a malicious tendency which would lead to vexatious acts. Can be a good friend or a good enemy. Be careful of your temper. Keep it under control. "The poison of asps is under their lips." Rom. 3:13.

G. No. 7 Hieroglyphic—Adder—Viper. Harbors revenge. The consequence of this is best expressed by: Proverbs 23:32, "At last it biteth like a serpent and stingeth like an adder." A disposition to return injury for injury. Personal vindictiveness. If victor over these, then the eternal triumph of intelligence and justice shall be yours. "Adder poison is under their lips." Psalms 140:5.

H. No. 8 Hieroglyphic—Sieve. Analytical. Logical. Power of reason. Capable as a chemist. Logician or literary critic. Capable of analyzing character at a glance. Intuitive. Can resolve things into their first principles, as in analysis of any proposition. Enjoys minute and critical examination of things. "I will sift the house of Israel among all nations, like as corn is sifted in a sieve." Amos 9:9.

I. No. 9 Hieroglyphic—Parallels. Lover of justice. Fair. Reasonable. Honest. Would succeed in any position where these qualities are needed. Clear conception of right and wrong. Devotion to principles of truth and facts. Impartiality. Cor. 8:14, 15.

J. No. 10 Hieroglyphic—Harp. Lover of harmony and peace. Idealist. Longing after things which exceed ordinary reality. Has high standard of excellence as an ultimate object of attainment. Makes constant endeavor to reach perfection. Chron. 25:3.

K. No. 11—Hieroglyphic—Bowl. Good provider. Loves plenty. Not satisfied unless there is abundance in sight. Cannot be content with daily allowance. Must have more immediately available. Fear of want. Must make provisions for future needs. Eccl. 16:6, 7.

L. No. 12 Hieroglyphic—Lioness. Lover of home and country. Patriotic. Courageous. Firm in decisions. Calm in face of danger. Brave, with great fortitude. Can trust only those who have been tried. Easy to get homesick. Longing for times that are gone. Job 38:39.

M. No. 13 Hieroglyphic—Owl. Shrewd. Keen insight. Sagacious. Careful thinker. Knowing without learning. Quickness of insight and discernment. Clever, keen and practical in most matters. Isaiah 34:11-15.

N. No. 14 Hieroglyphic—Water Sign. Very agitated, or very calm. Constantly thinking over private or public questions. Must be busy, or lose interest. Then inactive and destitute, becoming satisfied with things as they are. Always at extremes. Never medium. Rev. 15:2, 3.

O. No. 15 Hieroglyphic—Heart. Lovable. Affectionate. Kind. Has strong complex emotions. Delights in and craves the presence of objects of love. Strives to promote the welfare of loved one. Gentle; tender and good-hearted. St. Peter I 3:4.

P. No. 16 Hieroglyphic—Shutter. Secretive. Diplomatic. Deceptive. Loves to keep apart from others. Confides in no one. Close-mouthed. Will not give reason for actions. Tactful. Shrewd. Cunning. Inclined to act and say that which will deceive. Prov. 4:27.

Q. No. 17 Hieroglyphic—Knee. Reverence. Veneration. Obedient. Respectful. Feels profound respect for higher things. Adores that which is sublime, such as vastness, grandeur and power. Loves to comply with and be obedient to law. Rom. 11:4.

R. No. 18 Hieroglyphic—Moon. Romantic. Changeable. Unstable. Loves to indulge in visionary and fanciful things. Constant changing from one thing to another. Unsettled. Easily confused. Disturbed by surrounding conditions. Psalms 114:19.

S. No. 19 Hieroglyphic—Garden. Loves nature. Longs for outdoor life. Does not like things produced by man. Prefers that which is natural. Also that which is native to home and country.

Enjoys best things that are natural and primeval. "My country, 'tis of thee I sing," is the dominant sentiment. Ezek. 28:13.

T. No. 20 Hieroglyphic—Lasso. Desires to take. To own. To possess by putting forth exertion. Or to gain possession by force or strategy as in war or conquest. To guide or lead others in such conquest. To have direction or control of expeditions for discovery or prospecting. James 4:1.

U. N. 21 Hieroglyphic—Asp. Natural psychic. Able to read the history of things or persons by contact, or from objects with which they have been associated. Interested in occult phenomena of all kinds. Should engage in psychic research.

V. No. 22 Hieroglyphic—Asp. Clairvoyant. Second sight. Possesses preternatural knowledge. Capable of seeing that which is not visible to the normal eye. To foresee the future. Foretell events.

W. No. 23 Hieroglyphic—Harp. Loves music. Life of harmony essential to health and success. Rhythmic combinations of conditions and circumstances necessary to happiness. Order. Agreement. Conformity and unity of action must be present in both busines and domestic relations.

X. No. 24 Hieroglyphic—Chair. Loves authority. Has creative powers. Loves to command and force obedience. Longs for personal power that commands respect and confidence in others. Desires to create new laws and rules of action, and to have the power to enforce them.

Y. No. 25 Hieroglyphic—Tree. Loves music of nature. Given to sublime visions. A trusting nature that loves the tones produced by the winds, the sea, and the storm. In these, fancies he sees unreal and imaginary forces and things that come to the aid in bringing success and happiness. Deut. 20:29.

Z. No. 26 Hieroglyphic—Duck. Given to cringing and dodging the issue. Yielding. Hasty in action. Cowardly. Servile because of fear of the unknown. Surrenders too easily to the opposition of others. No fixedness of purpose. Allows circumstances to control. Acts without due consideration. Quick tempered. Impetuous. Irascible.

As the Master finished describing the influence of the various hieroglyphics on human life and character, he motioned the others to follow.

Then two of the Masters led the way down a long narrow passage which became lighter and brighter until it seemed the rock walls gave off a glow of whiteness such as can only be described as clear, white moonlight.

Finally we came to a beautiful throne, seemingly carved from the rocks by a skilled artist. The Master who was walking with the writer politely excused himself, walked to the Throne and said: "This is the Throne of Karma. It is in fact, the hieroglyphic from which man derived his idea of kingdoms, principalities and powers. The four doors we opened and closed as we came into the cavern are symbols of life and death. The first one, which opened outward, represents birth. It came into being as a part of a pre-existent living thing of its own kind, which has passed away. The two doors which close together from opposite sides of the hall-way symbolize the male and female. The one on the right side with a small door in it, typifies the mother principle. The one on the left with a cross upon it is the father—the burden bearer. The large door with the letter C and a cross upon it, symbolizes the union of the two in marriage.

"By consulting the foregoing table of hieroglyphics you will note that our English letter S is derived from a "Garden," where beautiful and useful things—'pleasing to the sight and good for food' are grown. In the word CROSS this letter is used twice, or doubled, expressing *abundance*."

[56]

The Master continued his explanation and told me that the form of the letter S itself indicates a planting and a coming up from the ground—Gen. 2:8, 9. Likewise in the word DOOR, the letter O is used twice, or doubled. This letter is derived from the hiero-glyphic "Heart." By consulting the above table it will be seen that the idea or symbolism of this letter is "Love." Indeed, this is the world-wide conception of the symbol. The form of the O being a circle indicates eternal life, and since it is doubled, this life is in two parts—here and hereafter.

THE CABIN

THE DOUBLE DOORS

THE DOOR WITH CROSS

THE STONE THRONE

THREE TIBETANS SITTING IN MOUNTAINS

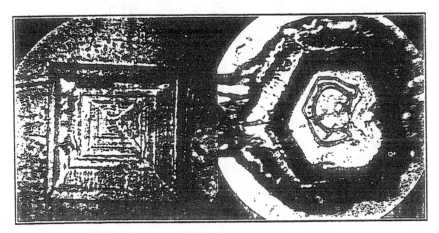

CHARACTER BUILDING—On the Square
By Letters in Given Name

SECOND INITIATION—Hindustan

Chapter V

Second Initiation—Hindustan

IN the early part of 1919 the writer published a book on his re search work: "The Beginning and the Way of Life." In this book he called attention to the harmony between the laws of life in nature as demonstrated by experiments in his own laboratory, in which life forms were produced anew from chemicals. These experiments verfiied the doctrine of the creation and formation of living things as recorded in the first and second chapters of Genesis.

At a later period, that is in 1922, while making further experiments in fixing mental pictures in mineral salts, such as were used in producing life forms, it occurred to the writer to ask whether his book had met with divine approval. To this question the following answer was given in Greek: "Since you have testified for God, He will now honor you with royal riches and wisdom so that you may complete your work on earth."

A few days after this, another message was given as follows, also in Greek: "A Cherub will now be sent to instruct you in the mysteries of life and immortality." Then followed one picture a day, except Sunday, until the thirty-six symbols of the book of Revelations were fixed as mental pictures in the salts, from which they were photographed. It is to be borne in mind that these, like all the other mental pictures, were but one thirty-second of an inch in size. Because they were microscopic it would be impossible to change them in any particular.

It was to these messages that reference was made by the Master during the first initiation, when he spoke of the writer's credentials which the Masters had received.

The "Seal and Signature of the Cherubim" which these credentials bore was the mental-picture of a dove with a man's hand under its wings. This is the same seal and signature that was given to Ezekiel. Ez. 1:8; and 10:20, 21.

For the second initiation the writer was taken on an astral journey, as he had been on the first night, but on this occasion he was taken to Hindustan. The scene of the ceremonies dated back to the time when all of India was called Hindustan. The location was near the town of Cawnpur on the upper Ganges. It was the imperative duty of all Hindus to bathe in the sacred waters of the Ganges, one of the greatest rivers of Asia. The dying were brought to the banks of this stream, in the belief that all who drank of its waters were exempt from the necessity of returning to this world and commencing a new life. These tenets of their religion are referred to here so that the reader may better understand why they were made a part of the initiation.

The second initiation was in Raja Yoga, which means Soul Consciousness.

When a candidate makes application for entrance to the School of the Magi, he is given a series of tests to prove his absolute reliance upon the powers of the Masters. These tests are made a part of every initiation. The candidate is first told that he must cast aside the erroneous conception that the physical body is the real self. The second initiation is intended to illustrate this. Until the candidate has mastered this instruction, or at least until this truth is fixed in his consciousness and he fully realizes that the body is no part of his actual identity, he is not permitted to take the third initiation. Often many incarnations elapse between the first admission and initiation, and the third initiation which admits the candidate to Mastership.

The writer's first impression of being in Hindustan was when he became conscious of the presence of the same three Masters he had met the night before in Tibet. He saw them standing near the main entrance of a wonderful Amphitheatre.

The beauty of this huge structure cannot be put into words. Its walls, embellished with every kind of precious stone, seemed to reach upward and blend with the azure of the star-lit skies. The full moon, just rising in the East, cast its pale yellow beams upon the waters of the Ganges. Even at that hour of the night, pilgrims could be seen bathing in the sacred waters, or assisting the sick and afflicted to do so.

As the writer surveyed this strange scene he turned to look at the faces of the Masters. He was unable to detect in their expressions either pity or compassion. But every few minutes one or another of them would lift his hand toward heaven and follow its motion with his eyes, as though watching some ascending object.

The writer tried to see what the Masters saw, then one of the number stepped to his side and said: "You are trying to see what we see, and you shall." Instantly there appeared to the writer's astonished gaze a host of angelic forms coming down from above, apparently intent upon meeting, and greeting, those who were just then leaving their now lifeless bodies on the banks of the sacred stream.

"This heavenly host," the Master explained, "as well as this great multitude of earth, have gathered here to attend your initiation into the science of Raja Yoga. This scene is the first part of the ceremony. It was ordered at this time for this purpose."

The writer ventured to ask: "Did you know beforehand that so great a number of souls would depart this life at this time?"

Scarcely had the question been formed in his mind before the Master answered: "All things are ordered beforehand."

After a moment of silence the Master continued: "The keynote of this initiation is: The Oneness of All. We wish first to impress upon your consciousness that we do not teach that you or I, or anyone, is God, or a part of God, or that it is possible to become gods. Such teaching is erroneous and misleading. It is a perversion of the pure Yogi teachings. This false doctrine has taken possession of many Hindu teachers, as well as in your western world. This is not the teaching of the School of the Magi. You will find no true Yogi teacher using the "I" in developing consciousness of the real self. We never use the "I." Neither will you do so when you are made a Master. We mention this at this time that you may hereafter avoid this "I am God" pitfall which awaits everyone just starting upon the journey to the Inner Temple. How could there be a Oneness of All and at the same time an "I am"? This belongs to God alone. In Him we live and move and have our being—our Soul Consciousness. This will be made manifest."

The interior of the amphitheatre was, if possible, more beautiful than the exterior. Around its great circumference were tiers of seats, as high as the eye could see, filled with an expectant multitude. The whole interior was lighted by smokeless, heatless torches burning with ribbon-like flames that would wreathe themselves in and out among the throngs like streams of red and white fleecy mists.

A massive chair with high, narrow back, and a large golden laver stood in the center of the great circular walls. Across the chair was a black robe, and on the back of the chair hung a Turkish fez. The writer was told to put these on, as no one was allowed to touch them. Not until then did the writer observe that the Master with whom he had been in conversation also wore a fez. The instant he was invested in these garments, some unknown force lifted and gently seated him in the chair.

As the writer looked out upon that vast audience, apparently without movement or sound of any kind, a strange sense of identity with them quickened his consciousness.

In front of his chair, and slightly below him, stood the golden laver. Its outer surface was beautifully ornamented with engravings of every known form of life. These began at the lower edge with the lowest types and seemed to progress in three concentric circles until the upper row contained models of the human form such as no sculptor of earth could have reproduced.

The laver itself contained a crimson fluid similar in appearance to freshly-drawn blood. It was in constant motion, dividing its surface into six-sided facets. As the writer watched these geometric figures, he observed that the plane of the upper surface of each was inclined at a different angle, so that each reflected a separate section of the great throng that seemed to be waiting in breathless silence. The formations in the laver would begin near the margin, then the completed figure with its mirrored group would be pushed toward the center by the formation of new facets at the outer rim. As the first ones moved nearer and nearer to the center, their reflected image would merge into a single human form. When they finally reached the center, each facet would in turn blend itself and its composite form into one,—common to all. And this one human form became the conscious soul of the writer, united with his physical body in an incorruptible whole.

As the writer meditated upon this marvelous illustration, he wondered why they, of whose blood he was, should spill his blood in war. "For God has made of one blood all nations to dwell on the whole face of the earth."

While these thoughts were passing through his mind, the Master with whom he had conversed, leaned forward and whispered a question: "Do you feel that if your life were in danger you could call to your aid this great army of watchers?"

At once, without considering that there might be one among the number who would not respond in case of necessity, the writer nodded in the affirmative.

Then came the crucial test.

The Master then said: "No fear, no harm. There will be loosed behind you a large, hungry leopard, holding a live cobra between its jaws. Should you show the least desire to escape by making the slightest movement, the leopard will drop the serpent and attack you. This will not only endanger your life, but also endanger those present. Thousands of our people lose their lives yearly through the cobra's bite. It is the most dreaded of all reptiles."

This warning had scarcely been uttered when there was heard the slow, soft tread of the big cat. As it approached, the writer could also hear the hissing of the struggling serpent. Presently the beast was so close that he could have laid his hand upon its back. Then the strangest of all human emotions took possession of him. He did not fear that he would be attacked, but rather he began to fear that they would not do so, and he waited in happy expectation of the sacrifice he was about to make in proof of his faith. As he waited breathlessly he became conscious that the leopard's tread and the hissing whistle of the snake were growing fainter, and presently he ceased to hear them.

As the writer meditated upon this, waiting rather in the hope than in the fear of death, the same unseen power that had placed him in the chair, now lifted him from it and placed him on his feet. He then noticed a six-headed figure carved in the side of the chair similar to those formed on the surface of the crimson fluid in the laver. It represented the six days of creation.

At this moment six trumpet bearers in pure white robes appeared and stood in a circle around the golden laver. The unseen power placed a trumpet in the right hand of the writer. The Master then announced: "We have chosen the Seventh Trumpet Bearer. Each will sound his number by the corresponding number of blasts." One, two, three, four, five, six, were then sounded by each trumpeter, according to his number until twenty-one blasts were blown. They then paired off in groups of two each. One group stood at the end of the laver opposite the chair, the other two on each side of it. Given in numbers, the pairs were made up as follows: Six plus one equals seven; five plus two equals seven; four plus three equals seven.

After a few words of instruction from the Master, the writer placed the mouth piece of his trumpet to his lips, and elevated its body in the air preparatory to sounding the next number, which would have been seven. The Master then extended his hands toward the multitude and said: "Here on the banks of this mighty River Ganges, while the full moon lingers above us at the zenith in the heavens, we invite the world to a realization of soul consciousness—the sacred science of Raja Yoga—which is the unutterable voice of the Seventh Trumpet."

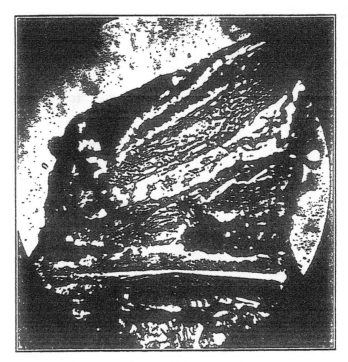

THE UPPER GANGES RIVER

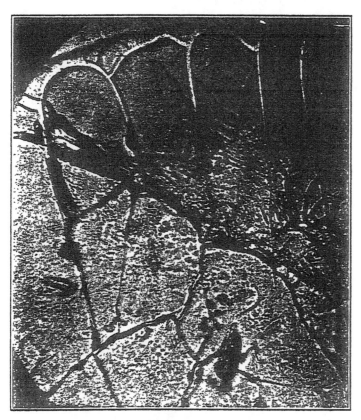

SEAL OF EZEKIEL

Mantra: The	Flying	Dove	Spirit	Seal
	1	1	1	1

"In Him We Live and Have Our Being"

GOD—EARTH

SIX CREATIVE DAYS

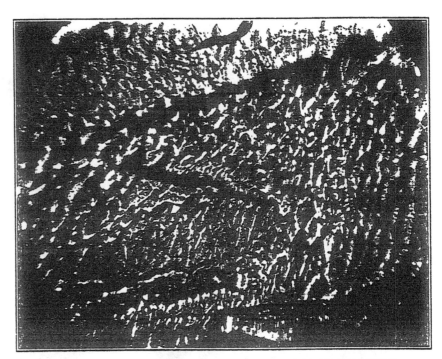

THE HEAVENLY HOSTS SEEN ABOVE GREAT THEATRE

THE GREAT TEMPLE NEAR RIVER GANGES

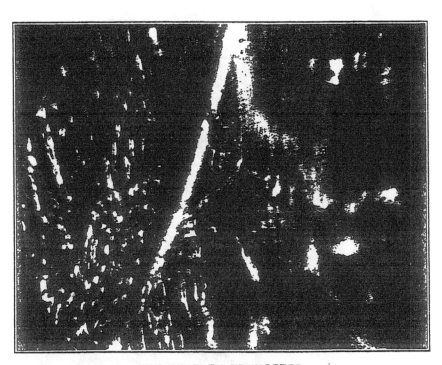

THE SEVENTH TRUMPETER

Mantra:	Trumpet	Curtain	Life
	5	5	5

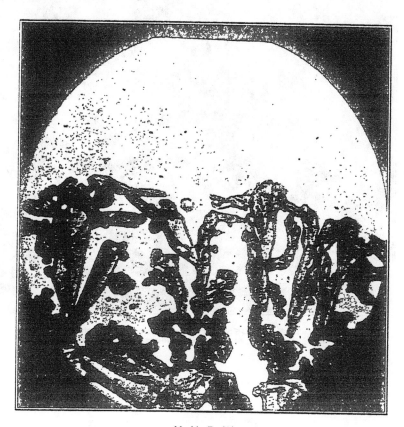

V. Y. P. W.

Mantra: Veda	Yogi	Pyramid	Wisdom
5	2	5	2

THE GOLDEN LAVER: Smokeless Torches
Center: Leopard with Cobra in its Jaws

80

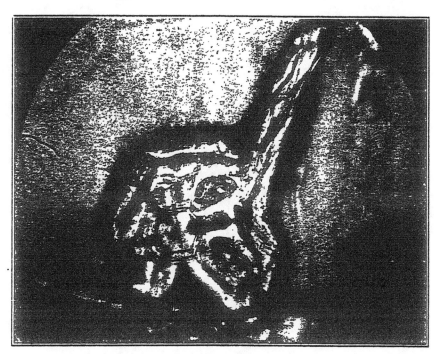

THE INITIATION CHAIR

THIRD INITIATION—EGYPT
TEN TRIANGLES
THE TWO CUBES

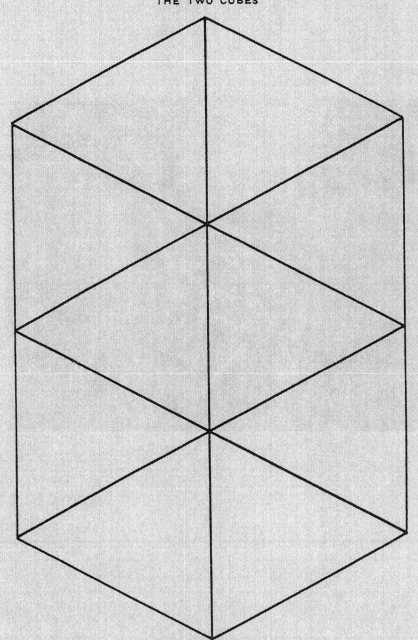

HERMETIC AXIOM:
"As Above, So Below. As Below, So Above."

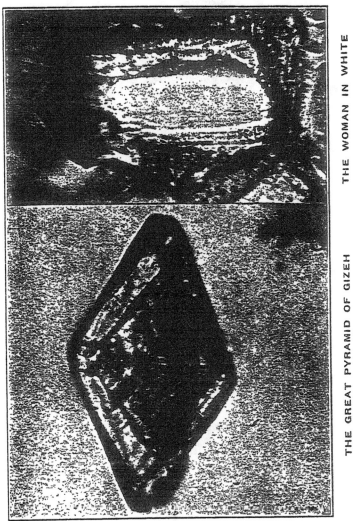

THE GREAT PYRAMID OF GIZEH

THE WOMAN IN WHITE

10 TRIANGLES: THE SERPENT

Chapter VI

HISTORY—PROPHECY—BY PERSONAL NUMEROLOGY

Third Initiation—Egypt

ON the third night the writer was taken to Egypt where he met, near the Great Pyramid of Gizeh, the same three Masters who were present at the former initiations. With them was a woman robed in folds of glistening white. The fabric of this garment appeared diaphanous, but it was not transparent, and seemed to be of a cloud-like texture. Her appearance suggested the essence of purity and wisdom. About her shoulders was a veil that draped itself in transverse folds to her feet.

This being was tall and slender with delicate, graceful hands, and when she moved there was a certain rhythmic flow to her body that was fascinating to observe. Her features were finely modeled and somewhat classic in appearance, but with a greater warmth and sympathy than the classic type suggests. Her skin was fair with a peculiar translucent quality, and her eyes deeply blue, lighted by a kindness and understanding not mortal.

When this angel spoke, for she was an angel in very truth, her voice seemed to echo and re-echo in the folds of her veil in musical tones not heard on earth.

After a moment's study of the writer, during which she seemed to be probing the depths of his soul, the angel said: "He is worthy." At this she drew from the folds of her veil ten flat-surfaced, silver-colored triangles, each of which bore a number. These triangles she laid on the ground, grouped as shown in the diagram which precedes this chapter. When the triangles were arranged, a serpent formed beneath them. As its head turned to look at the writer, the tail described a circle, the symbol of life. Then the angel chose one of the triangles, saying:

"This is the oldest symbol in the world. It is the pattern after which all things are fashioned. It is the idea. It is the word that expresses the idea. It is the image born of the word. By it all things were made, and without it was not anything made that hath been made. It is the universe of life and matter. Ten of these triangles, grouped as shown, form a perfect diagram of the Hermetic axiom: 'As above, so below. As below, so above.' "

As the angel ceased speaking, two of the Masters stepped to one side of the path, the third Master and the writer to the opposite side, which indicated that she would lead the way into the Great Pyramid of Gizeh. This she did by a secret passage beneath the great Sphinx.

Upon entering the passage the first Master and the writer were directed to follow the angel at a distance of ten feet. The other two Masters were instructed to follow us at the same distance.

The passage was probably ten feet wide and the same in height. We had proceeded about fifty feet when the angel halted, and turned to face us, raised her right arm above her head with the index finger pointing upward, and remained in that position while the first Master handed the writer a black robe, a long white apron, and a head-dress such as he never had seen before.

As the Master gave the writer these different garments, he explained:

"These garments are made of imperishable material. They were last worn by Yima when he was dedicated king of the golden age. May you preserve them free of spot or blemish." He waited until the writer was clothed in the different garments, then continued:

"We are now standing directly under the head of the Great Sphinx. Let me draw a word picture for you: Imagine a perfectly sculptured image of a lion's body one hundred and forty-six feet in length, with the strong grip of his paws extending fifty feet from his shoulders, which are thirty-six feet across; the whole surmounted by a proportionately sized intelligent human head, twenty-eight feet from the point of the chin to its top. Then ask yourself if the greatest human intelligence united with the greatest animal strength, appeals to your sense of logic as a prologue to an age-old prophecy of your country, the United States of America, and its mother country, the British Empire. The first has given to the world all the great modern inventions. The second has and will retain supreme power. The two were destined, long ages before the flood, to be and become the intellectual and physical powers of the earth."

When he had ceased speaking the angel lowered her hand, and touched her index finger to her lips, indicating *silence.*

Seven words, in tones of thunder, came from the bottomless pit beneath that massive symbol of the world's future glory, and reverberated along the passage.

So impressive was the experience that the writer was compelled to drop to his knees and bow his head to the floor. When the mighty reverberations had echoed and re-echoed through the underground corridors, finally to pass out through the head of the Great Sphinx, he raised his eyes and found himself alone.

"Thou Are Being Weighed In the Balance."

Had it not been for those seven words indelibly impressed upon his consciousness, he would have immediately retraced his steps. But their memory compelled him to go forward down the dark passage beneath that colossal structure. As he carefully groped through the darkness, feeling the wall with his right hand as a guide, he thought of the unspeakable words St. Paul had heard when caught away to the third heaven; of the voice of the seven thunders heard by St. John, but which he was not permitted to record, and wondered if they were the same thundering tones which had just re-echoed through that long corridor.

While he meditated on these things his eyes caught what appeared to be a very small cube of light far down the passage. What pitfalls might be between himself and that light he had no means of knowing. The Seven Words drew him on and on. Clearer, brighter, and larger became the light. At last it stood before him as though to block his progress. It filled the entire passage from wall to wall and from floor to ceiling.

The light did not move, and the writer also stood still. The only change, as the minutes passed, was in its brightness. It would grow dim and almost fade, then suddenly glow, clear and brilliant. These changes affected the vision, and it was impossible to see beyond the light. Finally the writer determined to attempt to pass through it. As he drew nearer, it seemed to go down and down into the center of the earth. When he raised his eyes, the light appeared to reach up into the sky. As he glanced to the right, he saw that the light appeared to extend an interminable distance. It also extended off to the left in the same way. Yet in the passage it remained a perfect cube.

Determined to test the nature of this light, the writer stepped into it, and instantly felt a gentle breeze which appeared to come from the direction from which he had come; also from the direction he was moving, but he could not feel the breeze to the right or to the left. At the cube the two currents met and turned upward.

On careful examination of these phenomena the writer believed that he had discovered how the builders of this first of the world's seven wonders had ventilated and lighted these underground corridors. Also the secret of the seemingly vast distance imparted to the eyes. When he looked to the right he could see himself approaching from a great distance. When he looked to the left, he could see himself going farther and farther away. These phe-nomena were not so easy to explain as were the others.

As he stood gazing in amazement at what appeared to be his own body approaching from one side of the passage and leaving it on the other side, he heard a human voice from the opposite direction from which he had come. The angel and the three Mas-ters had preceded him here while he had been listening to the re-verberation of the seven words of thunder.

As they entered the cube of light, the angel smilingly remarked: "We were just showing you yourself coming and going in your different incarnations, past and future."

Then as she stood near the center of the cube, her right arm extended above her head, the index finger pointing upward, the first Master spoke:

"Here in the midst of the land that was once called Egypt, in the center of the now land surface of the earth, on the exact dividing line between the northern and southern hemispheres, this cyclo-pean prophecy in stone was built by the people of the new earth, while they were yet of one language and one speech. That lan-guage and that speech was then that which we now know as the hieroglyphic source of the English language.

"They then knew more of mathematics, of geometry, of the laws of physics and of astronomy than is now known. And above all, they knew that which the Masters are trying to teach the world: *the mental control of matter.* It was through that power that these massive stones were put in place. It is that by which mankind will bring upon earth the reincarnation of the *thirteenth* Ji-van-muk-ti, or Golden Age of Yima."

Bowing to the angel he continued: "We beg the indulgence of your Majesty while we read a short message sent to the candidate in the year 1925, as the world records time. We will then invite his attention to certain scientific and historical facts which prove that this oldest and greatest existing monument of intellectual man was erected in prophetic anticipation of his country, and his people, who will, in the very near future trace their origin back to Egypt.

"On May 5, 1925, the following message was ordered: 'We, the Galileans are authorized by the Redeemer, Lord of Truth, this Seventh Age of Yuga, to number you 17,808 of Yima for the fourteenth *Ji-van-muk-ti*, Charles Wentworth Littlefield. Invested thou art. Inscribed from Hindustan by Eylil in Zansar.'

"For the benefit of the candidate we may say that all history and all prophecy are recorded in the astral world by a number code. These numbers never go beyond nine; ten is the infinite. Hence everything knowable by mankind comes under the nine digits.

"This first great pyramid was built to a scale of 9 feet perpendicular to 10 feet horizontal. For every 9 feet rise from its square base, it inclines inward 10 feet to a common center. But this rise upward and inclination inward is not abrupt, but gradual. Its name indicates the plan of construction. Pyramid is a combination of *Pyr*, which means division, and *met* which means ten. Hence the meaning of Pyramid is "Division of ten." Accordingly, a system of *fiveness* runs through the whole structure. This, the number code of the astral world shows to be the number of life.

"The *thirteenth*, or Golden Age of the Hindu chronology ended 17,808 years ago. This was centuries after the pyramid was built. The reincarnation of this *thirteenth* golden age began when the *thirteen* original colonies met in Philadelphia and by the act of their *thirteen* representatives signed and adopted the Declaration of Independence on July (the 7th month) A. D. 1776.

"Afterwards a national flag with *thirteen* stripes and *thirteen* five-point stars on an azure field, was adopted by the national congress. The signature of the *thirteen* who were the colonial representatives, which were affixed at different times to the Articles of

Confederation were secured in the following order:

"(1) New Hampshire, (2) Massachusetts Bay, (3) Rhode Island and Providence Bay, (4) Connecticut, (5) New Jersey, (7) Pennsylvania, (8) Delaware, (9) Maryland, (10) Virginia, (11) North Carolina, (12) South Carolina, and (13) Georgia. Your history shows this to be the exact order in which the *thirteen* delegates signed the original *unanimous* Declaration of Independence, and shows also that this is the exact order in which their former sovereign, King George III, acknowledged these thirteen original colonies to be free and independent States.

"Following this order, whether we count from left to right or vice versa, Pennsylvania is the *seventh* or center state, and has always been called the 'Key Stone State.'

"Afterwards the Congress adopted the Great Seal of the United States. This has on its obverse side an eagle bearing on its breast a shield of *thirteen* pales. From its beak flows a streamer on which are the words: E Pluribus Unum, which words contain just *thirteen* letters, and which means: 'Many in One.' Above its head is a blue sky within a cloud-wreath containing thirteen five-point stars. In the left talon it holds *thirteen* spears, and in the right, an olive branch with *thirteen* leaves. On the *reverse* side is a pyramid of *thirteen* courses of masonry built upon a single unbroken rock base. Above is: The All-seeing Eye within a triangle. Over the eye is the motto: *Annuit Coeptis*, in which there are also *thirteen* letters, meaning: 'God hath prospered our beginning.'

"This pyramid was built by the antediluvian people on the exact spot they knew would be the geographic center of the land area of the earth *after the waters of the deluge had subsided*. Before the flood there was no river Nile, no Mediterranean Sea, no Atlantic Ocean, no Pacific Ocean. In the place of the former ocean there was the continent of Atlantis; in the place of the latter, the continent of Pan. Since the flood the western mountains of Pan have been known as Je-Pan, meaning the sunrise. Before the flood there was no sunrise.

"In harmony with that which it indicates, this prophetic memorial, dedicated by a prehistoric people to the future race which they knew would come and reincarnate on earth a Golden Age similar to that in which they had lived, was built on *thirteen* acres of ground. For similar prophetic reasons they stopped just *thirteen* courses short of finishing it. This unfinished portion you will see in a vision."

With that, the writer and his four companions returned to the secret passage and emerged into the outer air. There again the angel spoke of the triangles, one of which she handed to the writer. "You will have published this eight years before this date," she observed smilingly, "according to personal numerology, which is the time-table of super-consciousness."

The writer did not then know the meaning of what he heard, and the presiding Master explained: "We shall presently understand what a remarkable prophecy she has made, and why things are pre-determined through a sequence of events which have their origin in some act of God or man. These may be foreknown by the science of personal numerology. It is my privilege and pleasure to illustrate by examples the operation of this law, not only in obliterating time as it is recorded in the physical world, but also showing you why certain promises of an endless life are made in your Bible, as well as in the scriptural writings of Tibet, Hindustan, and Egypt."

"It is asserted that the human body renews itself every seven years. This is not true," the Master smilingly denied. "The body *does* renew itself under normal conditions in the ratio, and at the periods calculated by personal numerology. If the individual will live in the super-conscious world, which is entered only by building power consciousness, attained through the comprehension of magical methods of computation of the . . . .

Veda	Yogi	Pyramid	Wisdom.	This formula controls
5	2	5	2	

the building power of the minerals of organic nature, and is known
by us as Personal Numerology."

| | 1 | | 1 | |

The Master then continued his explanation, of which the following is an outline:

How to Calculate Age and Foretell Events

Mantra	Table
415291	21235
22-4	13-4

1	2	3	4	5	6	7	8	9
A	B	C	D	E	F	G	H	I
J	K	L	M	N	O	P	Q	R
S	T	U	V	W	X	Y	Z	

A brief study of our English alphabet as placed above, with their
corresponding numbers from A to Z, gives the number of each
letter for use in the construction of a Formula, which, when meditated upon, will embody its *personal* or *spirit life power* in the mineral salts of organic nature as a mental-picture. For example, the
above words, personal spirit life power, which is a hebrew charm,
the numerical value of which is determined by adding the number
of the letters together until they are reduced to their lowest digit,
as follows:

Personal	Spirit	Life	Power
75916513	179992	3965	76559
1	1	5	5

The result of the above operation is called a Mantra. Thus:
7+5+9+1+6+5+1+3 equals 37 equals 10. 1+0 equals 1. So
we write the figure 1 under the word "personal." For the next word,
spirit, we have: 1+7+9+9+9+2 equals 37. 3+7 equals 10.

1+0 equals 1. So we write the figure 1 under the word "spirit." Next we have 3+9+6+5 equals 23. And the figures 2 and 3 added together made a total of 5. This number we write under the word "life." The fourth word has 7+6+5+5+9 equals 32. And 3 and 2 added together gives us 5. Our Mantra is completed by placing the number 5 under the word "power." See the picture of the ten triangles shown in the diagram at the beginning of this chapter.

It is not known beforehand what thought vibrations are set up by meditation on this mantra. So the writer places a drop of saturated solution of a mineral salt on the glass slide of the microscope, and while the water is evaporating from the drop, I meditate on the mantra formed.

When the water dries away the crystals of the salt are examined under the microscope. If an image of any letter, scene, person, bird, or animal is found, it is photographed with a microscopic camera. Then it is known that this mantra sends out the vibrations of that particular object or thing formed by the vibrations that group the particles of the salt. Then, if a sequence to the picture is desired, the name of the picture last received is embodied in another Mantra, which is also meditated upon as was the first. When the picture is formed and photographed, it is *always* a sequence of the first one.

From the above mantra a picture of the Persian crown was obtained—"The Crown of Life."

Then the following mantra was formulated:

Persian	Crown	of	Indian	People
7591915	39655		954915	756735
1	1		6	6

In other words the figures under the word Persian when added together made a total of 37. Then the 7 and the 3 were added, which gave a total of 10. And 1 plus 0 equals 1. So we place the figure 1 under the name Persian. The second word is 3+9+6 +5+5 equals 28. Then 2+8 equals 10. And again, 1+0 equals 1. So we place the figure 1 under the word Crown. Next we have: 9+5+4+9+5 equals 33 And then again, 3+3 equals 6. So we place the number 6 under the word Indian. We have next; 7+5+6 +7+3+5 equals 33. These two figures added together give a total of 6. This number is then placed under the word People, and our mantra is ready for meditation.

The drop of mineral-salt solution is placed on the glass slide of the microscope and allowed to evaporate in a temperature about that of the human body. When the crystals are formed there is found on the plate the head of an American Indian. We are thus inform-ed that this race of people came from Persia.

Then we write this mantra:

Had	They	Ordained	Government?
814	2857	69419554	7645954552
4	4	7	7

Here we have 8+1+4 equals 13. 1+3 equals 4. So we place the 4 under the first word. Then 2+8+5+7 equals 22. 2+2 equals 4. So the figure 4 goes under the second word, They. Then, as before: 6+9+4+1+9+5+5+4 equals 43. 4+3 equals 7. So we place a figure 7 under the third word, Ordained. Last we have: 7+6+4+5+9+5+4+5+5+2 equals 52. Then by adding the 5 and the 2 together, we have 7, which we place under the fourth word, Government, and our mantra is complete. Meditation on this Mantra produces the picture in the usual way. It is "The Corona-tion Chair." And we know that they were governed by a monarch.

In the same way any chapter of scripture may be formulated into mantras, and its historical or prophetic meaning obtained in mental-pictures. For example, in Revelation 10:1 and 2, we read: "And I saw another mighty angel come down from *heaven* clothed with a *cloud;* and a *rainbow* was upon his head, and his face was as it were the sun, and his *feet* as *pillars* of *fire.* And he had in his hand a little book open; and he set his right foot upon the sea and his left foot on the earth."

We have selected from these two verses, first, the scene; second, the actors; and third, the things heard and seen, and formulated them into mantras as follows:

First, the scene:

Earth	Sea	Rainbow	Cloud
51928	151	8195265	33634
25—7	7	37—10—1	19—10—1

Second, the actors:

Sun	Head	Hand	Feet
135	8514	8154	6552
9	18—9	18—9	18—9

Third, things heard and seen:

Voices	Thunders	Earth	Book
469351	28354591	51928	2662
28—10—1	37—10—1	25—7	16—7

1.

Hand	Above	Head
9	9	9

2. Opened book in hand of angel. Revelation. A message.
3. Right foot as pillar of fire, representing wisdom of white man.
4. Eagle and Shield.
5. Inside of little book held in hand of angel. Map of United States of America.
6. Left foot on earth wearing moccasin—the Indian's foot dress.

Personal	Numerology	in Name	Chronology.
1	1	6	6

The Master explained further by saying:

"In illustrating for our guest the use of this ancient system of computing ages, or as the Ancients called it, the 'Eye of God by Astral Ray,' may I request the consent of my brothers to use their names in doing this?"

As the Masters never spoke without first rising to their feet and making a very low bow, the first Master who presided over the initiation in Tibet arose and saluted the writer. Then the other one who was seated, and the one who presided remarked: "It is a very high honor to know that a memory of myself that goes far beyond a mere casual meeting or a lifetime acquaintance, but for my soul, is to be accepted, and in its very nature must become a part of his own soul-consciousness."

But to the surprise of the writer, he did not resume his seat, but remained standing. Then the Master who presided at the initiation in Hindustan arose, bowed to the writer, then to the other two masters, and said:

"My own soul will be enlarged, expanded, and made more beautiful, and will enjoy the consciousness of a wider, deeper and more enduring happiness if it can thus forever be associated with the soul of one so kind and self-sacrificing as our beloved guest." When he finished speaking, both Masters bowed very low to the writer, then to the presiding Master, and to each other, and were seated.

Nothing that can be said or written could express more fully and concisely the relation that this system of personal analysis creates between those who know each other by its reciprocal use.

"We shall now illustrate how the tabulated system of Higher Hieroglyphics, as presented in the first initiation in Tibet aids us in the development of superconsciousness in relation to the constant renewal of the body," the Master resumed, "and the limiting of extreme old age within the range of the laws of nutrition. By consulting this table we note that the first Master's initials are A. B. A being 1, and B, 2. The sum of these initials is 3, as indicated by the Mantra Table at the beginning of this initiation. Since this system of numerology can never go beyond 9, it is evident that Master A. B. lived seven years before the reversal of his superconscious age to 1 year of age again. Thereafter this reversal takes place every ten years. This period is known among the Masters as the New Birth.

"Let us suppose that he was born this year, 1926. (This was the date of the initiation." According to personal numerology we have 1926 as our base date; so we calculate: $1+9+2+6$ equals 18. $1+8$ equals 9. He will be 10 years old in 1936. This is now 1936, which added together equals 19. So, $1+9$ equals 10, or $1+0$ equals 1. So, in 10 years the Master A. B. has in his superconsciousness returned to 1 year old, or babyhood in his nutritive processes of renewal of his body.

"Let us now take 1937, when he will be 11 years old. $1+9+3+7$ equals 20 and 20 gives us 2. So in one year from the last date he will be two years old in the renewal process of his body, or superconscious vital powers.

"In 1938, or 12 years from his birth date, we have $1+9+3+8$ equals 21. $2+1$ equals 3. He will then be 3 years old in the renewal processes of the body. Although he will now be 12 years old from his birth from a material standpoint, yet he is only 3 years old in bodily renewal.

"Next we have 1939—$1+9+3+9$ equals 22. $2+2$ equals 4. He is now 4 years old in powers of nutrition. We next take 1940. $1+9+4+0$ equals 14. $1+4$ equals 5. He is now 5 years old.

"Next 1941. $1+9+4+1$ equals 15. And $1+5$ equals 6. He is now 6 years old in superconscious life. Next 1942. These figures added together give a total of 7. He is here 7 years old. Then in 1946, which totals 20, or, reduced to its lowest digit, gives us 2. Two years old in nutritive powers. This is exactly 20 years from his birth, yet he has a 2 year old nutritive power consciousness.

"From the initials of his name A. B. -3. When he has added

three ten year periods to his life it will be 1956, and $1+9+5+6$ equals 30. He will have reached the age of Mastership, as did Jesus.

"Our brother C. I.—$3+9$ equals 12 equals 3 corresponds exactly to the foregoing computation. I am Master I. B.—$9+2$ equals 11 equals 2. My own life, regardless of when or where I was born, would run through the same changes in the same period of thirty years. God is no respecter of persons, regardless of when or where they were born; but in every nation he that kept His law is accepted of Him."

Here the presiding Master resumed speaking. To the other Masters he said: "Our guest brings the number of our personal analysis up to ten thousand, which reminds me of the old song: "When we've been there ten thousand years bright shining as the sun, we've no less days to sing God's praise than when we first begun." Since 10,000 years is, in reality, only one year to super-consciousness, we can understand more fully the meaning of this and other Christian symbolism. To these we now invite the attention of our guest.

"Beginning with the announcement of the birth of Jesus to the Virgin Mary by the Angel Gabriel (Luke 1:26), the subsequent meeting of Jesus with his twelve disciples on Mount Zion (Matt. 5:1 to 10) where he taught them the ten blessings of discipleship, which he declared is the accomplishing of the law (not the Jewish law) in the living of the ten Mantras known as the Beatitudes: 'Is the Kingdom of Heaven." (Matt. 5:3).

| 1 | 1 | 1 |

Here we present our readers with full sized photographs of the life of Jesus, and the Mantras that were used in obtaining them as the Master described the scenes. Sometimes one mantra would produce two pictures showing vibratory harmony between them. In these, the second picture is placed above the first on the same page.

[99]

1.

CRUCIFIXION

Lamb Sacrificed for Man
1   3   3   1

2.

RESURRECTION.

Mental Mastery of Life Power.
2   2   5   5

3.

ASCENSION — ANNUNCIATION.

Now to your God.
7   8   7   8

4.

CHURCH.

Your Church of Life Masters.
7   7   5   5

5.

HOLY GRAIL.

Communion of His People.
9   3   9   3

6.

MOUNT ZION.

144,000 Symbolize Your Church.
9   9   7   7

7.

Church Duty Love World
7   7   9   9

8.

Eye of God   Astral Ray
8   8   8   8

Rev. 14:1.

[100]

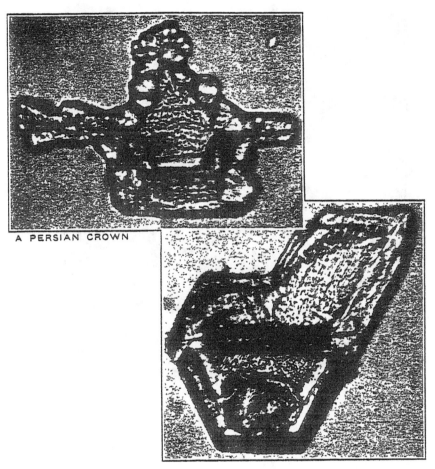

A PERSIAN CROWN

THE CORONATION CHAIR

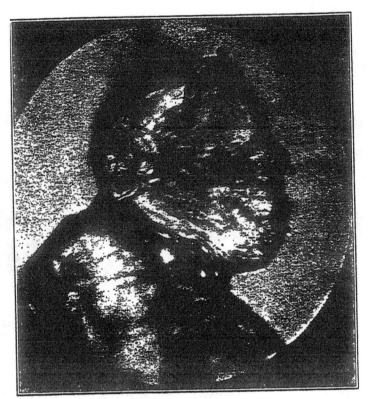

AN INDIAN HEAD

THE EAGLE AND SHIELD

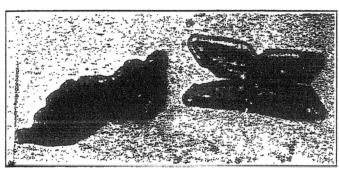

THE HAND ABOVE HEAD

103

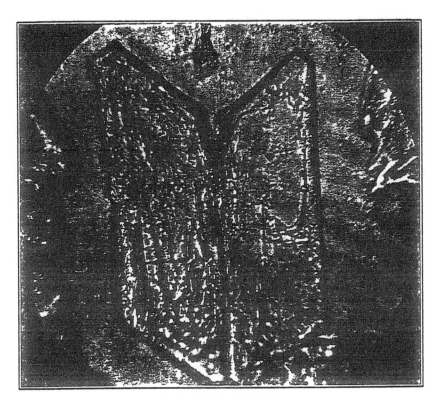

THE BOOK OPENED
(A Thought Picture)

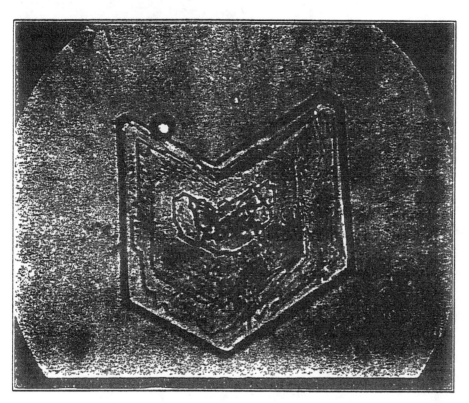

THE INSIDE OF THE BOOK
Map of United States of America

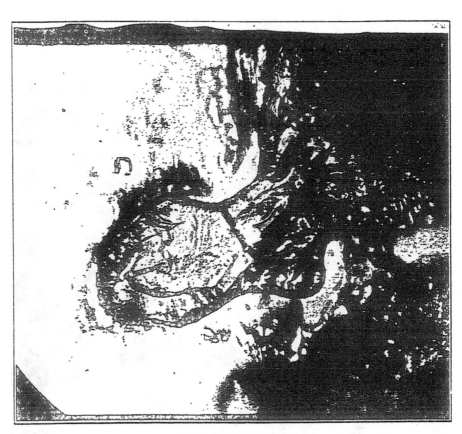

THE RIGHT FOOT
"And he set his right foot upon the sea." (Rev. 10:2)

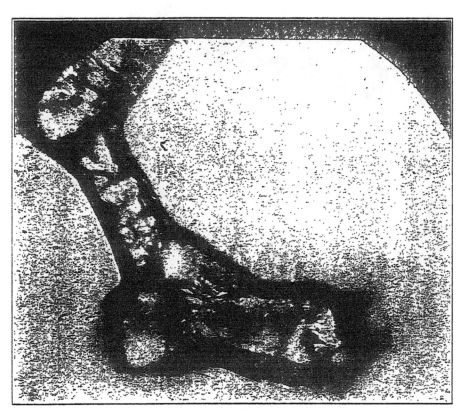

THE LEFT FOOT
"And his left upon the earth." (Rev. 10:2)

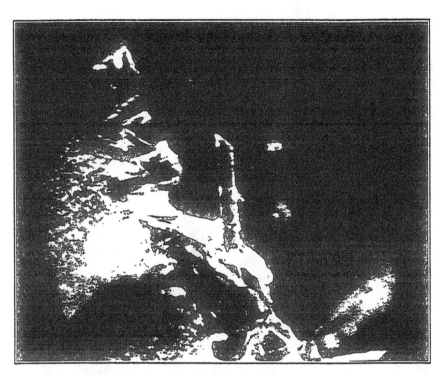

THE CRUCIFIXION. (Matt. 27:45
Mantra: "Lamb   Sacrificed   for   Man."
          1   3   3   1

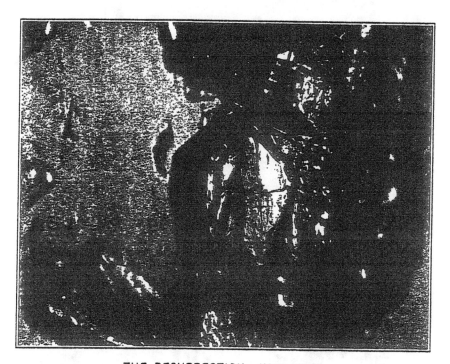

THE RESURRECTION. (Matt. 27:57)
Mantra: Mental Mastery of Life Power
        2   2   5   5

THE ASCENSION OF JESUS

Mantra:	Now	to	Your	God
	7	8	7	8

THE ANNUNCIATION. Matt. 1:13

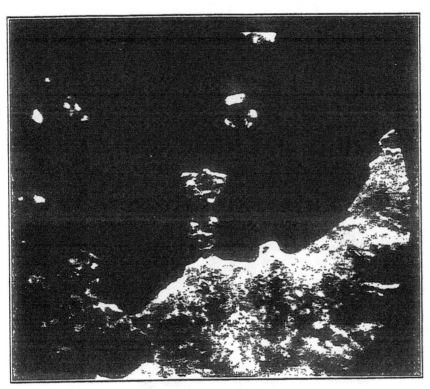

THE HOLY GRAIL OR CHALICE

Mantra: Communion of His People
$$\frac{Communion}{9} \quad \frac{of}{3} \quad \frac{His}{9} \quad \frac{People}{3}$$

THE RESURRECTION CHURCH

Mantra: Your Church of Life Masters
7 7 5 5

MOUNT ZION

Mantra:	144,000	Symbolize	Your	Church
	9	9	7	7

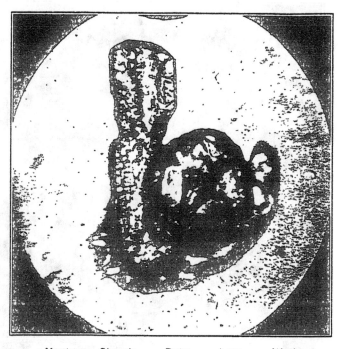

Mantra:	Church	Duty	Love	World
	7	7	9	9

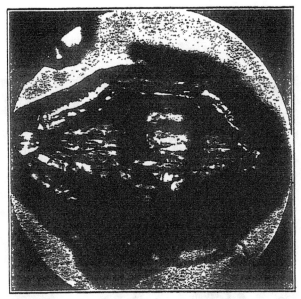

Mantra: THE EYE of GOD
       ——   ———
        8   8

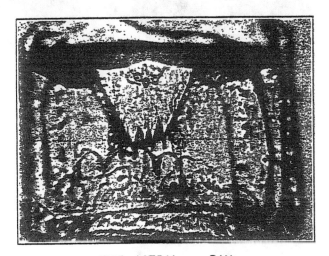

THE ASTRAL   RAY
          —   —
          8   8

Mantra: Astral   Ray   —   Eye   of   God
        ———   ———   ———   ———
         8   8   8   8

The above pictures were both produced by the same mantras.

THE "ROSY CROSS"

Mantra:	Rosy	Cross	Wisdom	Symbol
	5	2	2	5

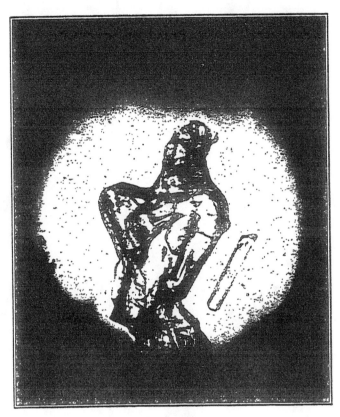

THE DOVE

Mantra:	Dove	Symbol	Life	Spirit
	1	5	5	1

Chapter VII

HUMAN PHYSICAL PERFECTION

THE writer's experiments demonstrate that every human being is *within* a potential store-house of all possibilities, requiring only the essential mineral salts to give practical expression to every desire of the human mind. Everyone is conscious of this fact, conscious of ability within which he cannot express, conscious that his immortal self (the mental-image) is capable of infinite development and equally infinite achievement.

This potential power for doing things lies solely in the mental-image, the spirit. The agency for directing this power in the desired channels, lies solely in the mind, while the power for executing these desires lies solely in the physical body.

These propositions being true, it follows that unless the individual finds himself the possessor of a physical body which enables him to achieve his highest ideals—the development of the body to meet the requirements of his mind—life for him, in a proportionate measure, must be a failure.

Now and then we meet a happy balance—one whose mind and body seem capable of parallel development to an unlimited extent. These are they who ascend the thrones of the world, and by these, all unbalanced individuals are controlled, whether they will or not.

Why is there such a difference between human beings? Why do some fail in body and mind at forty, while others remain active in business and social life at eighty? Why does one child in a family develop criminal tendencies while the other children are morally and spiritually inclined? Why is the life of one person blighted by this or that hereditary disease, while another, whose ancestors violated every law of God and man, go free? These questions have been asked by thoughtful persons many many times.

My answer involves, first, a distinct recognition of a potential psychic power due to ideals *fixed* in the mind of the mother and held sacred by her during the period of gestation. This I hold as having a most important share in directing the vital processes of the body, either for weal or woe, both before and after birth.

Second, the necessity of a constant supply to the blood, irrespective of the food we eat, of the proper grouping of the mineral salts to meet the daily needs of the tissues for growth and repair.

In this dual process lies nature's secret of that physical development necessary to meet every desire of the soul; to perpetuate life indefinitely, to maintain perfect health, and to sustain full mental and physical activity during the whole period of life. This answer to these most important questions of human life is not a matter of speculation, but on the contrary is founded upon exact scientific methods put into daily practice during a quarter of a century.

The problem of mineral starvation of blood and tissues has long engaged the attention of medical men. It is now generally recognized that this starvation underlies all diseases, and through weakening of the tissues makes bacterial invasion possible.

In order to bring clearly before the mind the importance of the mineral salts as the physical basis of life, I must enumerate the functions performed by them as demonstrated by the experiments of myself and others:

1. By their grouping and apportionment all vegetable and animal forms are determined.

2. They enter into the composition of every cell.

3. The mineral composition of cells determines the kind of tissues and organs they build.

4. As bearers of the vital force they give expression to all of life's functions.

5. They determine whether the vital force shall express motor, nutritive, sensatory, or volitional energy.

6. By doing this they govern the contraction of all muscles, including those of the heart.

7. They preside over the nutrition, growth and renewal of every part.

8. They connect the consciousness with the external world through the five senses.

9. They control the proportion and chemical combination of the five essential elements; oxygen, hydrogen, nitrogen, carbon, and sulphur, that compose the proteins, starches and fats of organic nature, building each kind, according to the species of plant and animal.

10. They are the basis of development of the organs of the brain, for the expression of different mental faculties.

11. They are the media through which the body develops in response to impressions made upon the vital force.

12. Finally, they give expression through the features to the intelligence, moral qualities, and emotions of the soul.

These, then, are some of the functions of the minerals salts of the body.

Considering their nature and importance, it is at once obvious that life could neither endure nor express its qualities, if its complex mineral requirements were not constantly maintained. These are the facts which warrant consideration of the subject of how to use the mineral salts in individual and race improvement and healing. It is my belief, based upon years of observation, that I have discovered the basis of exact quantitative control of the mineral requirements of the human body. If so, we may proceed in a scientific way to perfect humanity; prolong life indefinitely, and maintain all its functions unimpaired. This *basis* is that grouping of the mineral salts which built for me a human form.

I have already shown that when these mineral salts of organic nature are charged with the vital force, they become susceptible to mind control so that any picture the mind accepts as *true in principle*, may be fixed in them.

Not only will the vital force reflect through such "faith-pictures" our own preconceived beliefs by appropriate symbols, but it will also reproduce our conceptions of the features of a favorite author. One of my favorites, St. Paul, was shown to me in this way. This proves that the vital force has the power, or function, to use the mineral salts to express personality through the features. Why, then, may we not use them to express all other desires of the mind and soul, in business, in social life, and in our domestic relations?

When we come to study the operations of the vital force in the building and functional activities of living things, we find its office is, first, to endow living things with *physical* sensation, which may be defined as the power to respond to external stimuli. This power is possessed in some degree by every living thing, both in the vegetable and in the animal kingdoms.

The vital force of the vegetable kingdom responds to the various forces of the environment; light and color, heat and cold, storm and wind, all of which influence their growth, their development, their functions.

Agricultural chemists now know that unless a plentiful supply of the mineral salts of organic life is in the soil, plant life will not survive. They also know that more water is needed in the soil, than the amount required by the plant for its organic growth. Just why this is so they do not know. My discovery of the generation of the vital force by the evaporation of water, gives us the reason for this, and as heretofore shown, this evaporation must be at the same temperature as that which is normal to the growth of the plant.

The second function of the vital force is that of *voluntary motion*. This may be defined as the power of spontaneous movements and under this function we have all the expressions of attitude, of features and of form, of which the lowest or highest animal organisms are capable. This function of the vital force includes every movement; therefore, from a smile or a frown to the most strenuous physical exertion to express our feelings, either in pleasure, in work, or in defense. This impulse to voluntary movement may arise, either from a desire from within or from stimuli from without.

A third function of the vital force is that of attraction and repulsion among the particles it affects. These particles may be only small pieces of one of the mineral salts, or it may be organized forms as human individuals.

The law is "that every form of energy acts through some particular form of matter", as pointed out in my book: "The Beginning and the Way of Life." To this I may now add: The vital force of organic life not only selects the twelve mineral salts of organic nature through which to act, but it also selects some particular grouping of these salts for the expression of each of its several functions.

Not only are certain individuals of the same sex attracted or repelled by each other by these powers of the vital force acting through particular groupings of the mineral salts which determine the differences in individuals, but also persons of opposite sex are attracted or repelled for the same reason. This attraction and repulsion among plants and animals, in the psychic realm, is known as love and hate. This particular manifestation of the vital force is the most active in the constitution of the two sexes during the period when the generative function of each is in its greatest vigor.

The writer will show, in speaking of the law of heredity, that this *love* and *hate* is manifested or expressed through two particular mineral salts—phosphate of sodium and phosphate of lime. These relate particularly to the period of puberty when the boy is developing into manhood and the girl into womanhood. The change taking place at this time relates to the function of these salts, in the chang-

[123]

ing of the infant skeleton from a cartilaginous frame work, made up almost solely of sodium compounds, and the replacement of these by the lime compounds, which constitute more than seventy per cent of the adult skeleton. At this period the sodium salts that formerly constituted the skeleton of the child are now being used to develop its generative organs. If at this period there is an insufficient supply of lime, the sodium salts are not released from the skeleton, with consequent underdevelopment of the reproductive organs. Prior to this, indeed, during the period of gestation, the brain, with its several organs, is formed, and at birth each begins to exert itself over the growth of the different parts of the organism.

The growth of the brain always precedes the development of other parts of the body. The brain of an infant is, compared with the body as a whole, very voluminous, being in proportion of 1 to 8, while in adults it is 1 to 40 or 1 to 50. From infancy it grows rapidly up to the seventh year. The brain of an infant which weighs at birth three quarters of a pound, weighs at its second year nearly one pound and a half, and at its seventh year it attains a weight of more than two and a half pounds. During these years the individual mind is only slowly developing, and does not come into full activity until after the brain itself is fully developed.

If this fact teaches anything, it teaches that there are forces in nature that build organs to perform functions, and that these functions are the same forces that previously built the organ.

Among all created things, in strict accordance with the law of composition already stated, differences of form are found to be commensurate with differences of character and ability to do. Things which resemble each other in quality and function resemble each other in shape; and wherever there is unlikeness of quality and function there is unlikeness of configuration. It may be observed further, that whenever through *use* a change takes place in development of certain organs there is a corresponding change in character.

We are hardly permitted to doubt, therefore, that there is, in all cases, a determinate relation between the chemical constitution and the quality of service, although we may not always be able to trace it out.

The differences we observe among individuals are not accidental, nor are they mere arbitrary marks without meaning. There is a cause in the innermost nature of man, why each individual should possess a precise personality, and *this cause may be found in the mental state which dominated the mother during the period of gestation.*

The outer or physical man then, is but an image or material representation of the inner or spiritual man. The soul, modified in its manifestations by its physical fellow, and subject to constant impressions from without, *does*, nevertheless, build up the body *at will* to meet its changing character and wants, subject, of course, to the necessary supply of the required materials.

This mind-image of man, transmitted to him from the soul life of the mother, can only be *made perfect* by making the life of the mother one of perpetual happines and contentment.

This writer is neither a religious nor a political reformer. His message is based upon the one that has come down through the centuries from a *perfect physical man*, born of a virgin, dominated by a conception given to her by the Archangel of God. This message is here substantiated by exact science. He therefore lays before his readers his conception of the essential conditions necessary to surround every prospective mother with the consciousness of perpetual joy, to the end that man may again come into his rightful heritage of a perfect physical being. This, not only for the yet unborn, but also for those now living.

As a chain is no longer than its weakest link, so a city, state, or nation is no stronger than its weakest individual. We flatter ourselves that the majority rules, and that the average is the standard. Such is not the case.

A strong man, full of blood and vitality, has only the thinnest, transparent membrane, surrounding the large blood vessels of the brain, which are liable to rupture from the slightest cause and bring destruction and death to the entire organism. So a city, state, or nation, while not so *immediately* destroyed by affections of its weakest part, is nevertheless just as surely destroyed.

With the same certainty that the subtle unseen power of drugs acts upon the weakest parts of the organism, producing disease which finally pervades the entire body, so do the unseen, secret sins of a city, state, or nation act upon its weakest members, then spread to the entire community to finally destroy it.

As the hand, seemingly well, cannot say to the foot which is sick: "I am independent of you, and have no fear of being affected," nevertheless, just so surely as the foot is not healed, the hand will cease to be well. The vital-force of the hand is the same as that of the foot, and we cannot strike an average between the two, but the vitality of the hand will sink to that of the foot, and both will die if the foot be not healed.

There is just such a community interest in the standard of the vital forces in every city, state, or nation. If want and poverty pervade the lower strata of society, depleting the blood and brain of the twelve mineral compounds which build the body, thereby bringing on anxiety, sorrow, vexation, crime, think you the upper crust, made of the same materials, will escape the poisonous effects of this subtle influence? While the honest merchant and manufacturer is being ground down by the merciless trusts until the spectre of financial ruin robs him of restful slumber, do you think the sleep of the millionaire will be without a nightmare?

How often do we see men and women of means, and without a care in the world, commit suicide, because suicide arising from the

den and the brothel pervades the air? How often men of respecta-
bility commit theft in the midst of plenty, only because some hungry wretch has spent a sleepless night planning to rob a bank!
How often men and women of purest lives fall to the level of the
brute, only because the mistakes of others have been published
abroad, filling the public mind with the thought!

How often, Oh, how often these things occur, and the unhappy
victims remain ignorant of the cause! Will the world never learn
wisdom? Will it always be misguided? Think well before you
answer, for it shall be done as you and others decide. If you and
they prefer to choose aright, a new heaven and a new earth, with
new avenues to health and happiness shall be opened, the results of
which will transcend the hope of angels.

As the vital force which builds the body and its organs is inseparable from the matter with which it works, so the prevailing
thought of any city, state, or nation is inseparable from its moral,
commercial, and governmental conditions. As grouping in various
proportions of the twelve mineral compounds determines the species of the organism, so will the grouping and the apportionment
of thought determine the character and quality of a community.
Since no one of these minerals alone can build an organism, neither
can many different minds alone affect the moral, commercial, or
governmental status of the community. They must all think the
same thing at the same time, for the same purpose. In other words,
there must be perfect agreement of thought, and just as sure as a
man is as he thinks, just so sure is a city, state, or nation as it
thinks.

It is not sufficient that there is hope and desire for better conditions. There must be the active, impelling thought—the mental-
image—sent out daily from thousands of minds at the same time
for a single purpose.

[127]

We have a picture in the New Testament of a new church at work in this very capacity. In Revelation we find an account of the 144,-000 people being sealed in their foreheads, for the very purpose of delivering the world from great tribulation, after the "kings of the earth, and the great men, and the rich men, and the chief captains, and the mighty men," and all others had gotten the nations into such difficulty that many were killing themselves. and none were able longer to endure the tribulation, and were crying out for the mountains and rocks to fall on them and hide them from the face of the lamb.

But immediately after the sealing there was seen a great multitude, which no man could number, of all nations, and kindred, and people, and tongues, crying with a loud voice, saying: "Salvation, Salvation, to our God, and to the Lamb."

What could have wrought such a marvelous change? It was this 144,000, who were taught to think—to formulate a mental-image of this new age—and who were *sending this image daily* to the world on the vibration of the rainbow rays.

The mission of this book is to prepare this people. These will correct, by the mental-image they hold, every wrong in the social, commercial, and political life of the nation.

This will banish sickness, wipe the tears from every eye and bring an abundance of prosperity to every person. It will do more. It will convert our land into a paradise and, through the use of the twelve mineral salts, will lengthen the days of youth to an hundred years, and the fullnes of life to a thousand. Those who are ignorant of the power of the mental-image will regard the above statement as foolish. To all such the writer would commend a fair trial of the law before condemning it.

Chapter VIII

PRACTICAL INSTRUCTION

THE following instructions are offered to aid the amateur chemist, psychologist, metaphysician, or numerologist, who wishes to work out these experiments.

As a first step, a good microscope with not less than two objec- tives, one of low power that will take in the head of a common pin, the other of high power that will not take in the body of the pin, is essential. The body of a pin is 1-32 of an inch; the head, 1-16 of an inch, or just double the size of the body.

From a wholesale drug house procure one ounce or more of the twelve mineral salts, known as tissue salts. These are:

1. Sodium chloride.
2. Silicon (silicea).
3. Chloride of potash.
4. Fluoride of lime.
5. Sulphate of lime.
6. Sulphate of potash.
7. Phosphate of potash.
8. Phosphate of magnesia.
9. Phosphate of iron.
10. Phosphate of lime.
11. Sulphate of soda.
12. Phosphate of soda.

Procure twelve one ounce bottles with fresh, clean corks. Label each bottle with the name of the salt it is to contain. Into each bottle put about 10 grains of one of the salts and fill with pure distilled water. Shake frequently. Not all the salts are equally soluble, some in large amounts and others only slightly.

From time to time remove a drop of any one of the solutions

with a clean toothpick to the glass slide of the microscope. Place the slide near a small electric globe suspended from a cord over the table where you use your microscope until the water of the drop is evaporated. Then examine the crystal formed from the salt. Do this with each of the twelve salts until you become familiar with their forms and differences. Then combine two or more of the solutions in a clean bottle. Place a drop of this on the glass slide, then evaporate and examine.

It will be seen by these experiments that the slightest difference in the amounts of each solution will make the widest possible difference in the resulting crystals. These combinations may be varied to suit the fancy of the experimenter. They should be followed until it is fully demonstrated that the difference in quantity of the salts produces the wide variations chrystaline in form.

In my own experiments I use sulphate of potash and sulphate of soda, one part of the potash to ten parts of the soda. When this combination forms crystals like the letters C, D, or O, then the solution of these salts is susceptible to mental mastery by my mind. Whether this would yield to the mental state of others I do not know. Experiments can only determine this. Other combinations of different salts should be tried if this one does not produce results.

Building Mantras.

In the formation of mantras any statement or description of any scene may be chosen. Three of the words selected from it must agree in one number, or four of them may be of two different numbers. For example: "Veda Yoga Pyramid Wisdom" as given
5   2   5   2
by the Masters to indicate the system of philosophy they taught, composed of four words, two of which correspond to the same number. Or the mantra may be formed by a combination of numbers and letters, as the one for Mount Zion:

[130]

PRACTICAL INSTRUCTION

144,000	Symbolize	Your	Church.
9	9	7	7

The secret of their formation is: Embody your own ideas, or those of any member in a group, in such manner that the numbers are all the same, or two or four are both of the same number. Then meditate, or *think,* on them as elsewhere described.

Throughout this entire book the writer has tried to present in faithful detail the instructions received from the Masters. In all of this, including the mental-pictures formed in the mineral salts, there has been this thread of truth:

"And it was so."

Turn back for the moment to Genesis, Chapter 1, and read from the third to the sixth verse. There is the positive declaration—the affirmation. What happened? "God said: 'Let there be light'; and there was light." Here is the command, and the carrying out of that command. This is apparent all through this entire first chapter. Here is the mantra, then the coming into manifestation of the condition or the thing declared—the "mental control of matter," as the Masters pointed out. "And God said: 'Let the waters under the heaven be gathered together in one place, and let the dry land appear': *and it was so."*

Here it is shown very clearly that it is possible to bring into being the thing desired. In the writer's research it has been demonstrated over and over again, that when the mantra is taken into meditation, then the picture appears in the mineral salts.

In this connection, the writer again emphasizes the fact that these pictures are so tiny—one thirty-second of an inch when the picture covers the entire surface of the drop of solution. In many instances the *picture* occupies but a fraction, sometimes only *one-seventh* of the whole drop. There is, therefore, no possibility of tampering with the formations, nor any way of changing any detail. However skeptical the reader may be, there is no foundation for a charge

[131]

of fraud. Furthermore, by following the instructions given for the use of the microscope, as set forth in the beginning of this chapter, any inquiring student can secure adequate proof of mental control of matter.

It is also possible to use the mantra, the building of which has been explained in previous chapters, for meditation without the aid of the microscope and the mineral salts.

We are told in John 15:7: "If ye abide in Me, and My words abide in you, ye shall ask what ye will, and it shall be done unto you." This, indeed, is "speaking the word." This is the creation and formation which was so strongly impressed upon the writer by the Masters.

While using the mantra, it is well to set up a rhythm of three. That is, make your statement and repeat it three times, and again three times, until the condition or the thing you will to come into manifestation appears.

The writer does not deny that instant results have been obtained by petitions to God by those to whom personal numerology was an unknown science. There are times when the peril is too imminent to allow time for setting up a mantra. But if you cry out: "God help us," your plea is heard and your safety assured. The use of the mantra, however, worked out as shown, is merely working *with* the Law. When one knows the law, it is better to live it to the letter than to ignore it. Furthermore, there must be faith. You must *believe* that the thing you desire is *now* established. Whether its appearance is immediate or delayed makes no difference. The law is working for you and with you. You must know that the answer will come. This is a very important point and should never be lost sight of by the student.

It is well to remember that "Time is naught in the mind of God." While many appeals are answered instantly, we sometimes need to raise our own spiritual vibrations, awaken our soul consciousness, by daily meditation. If you can set a definite time each day to sit

[132]

down quietly for meditation, you will find that you are richly rewarded. This period may be anywhere from ten to fifty minutes. Vagrant thoughts should be driven from the mind and the whole consciousness centered upon the words of the mantra, or prayer.

Because of delayed manifestation, students often become discouraged. Keep in mind that the desire may require the adjustment of many other conditions, much as we put together the pieces of a picture puzzle. Perhaps the whole picture will have been completed before the odd piece can be fitted into its proper place.

To make this more clear, the writer recalls an experience related by a patient. She had been given a fine musical education as a girl, then had married, and across the ensuing ten years, there never seemed to be enough money to purchase that which she wanted most—a piano. Studying her Bible one day, she read again John 15:7. "Why shouldn't I have a piano? God owns everything. He has lots of pianos. There is no reason why He should not give one to me, His child."

This thought kept recurring through the following days. Somewhere she had read that if one declared a thing to be true, then it was made manifest. She thought of all the many, many promises in the Bible, and finally, knowing nothing of personal numerology, she made her declaration: "I have a lovely brown piano."

Thinking about her new piano, she reflected that a place should be made for it in the living room. When she cleaned and dusted the furniture, she also went through the motions of dusting and polishing the instrument she loved. During the ensuing weeks she never doubted that the piano would soon make its appearance in her home. Daily, not even knowing the word meditation, while she washed dishes, washed and ironed clothes, and performed her many household tasks, she kept repeating: "I have a lovely brown piano." In very truth it became a song in her heart.

The reader will note that this lady had, quite unwittingly, set up a mantra: "A lovely piano," gives the perfect number. The words:

$$\underline{A} \quad \underline{lovely} \quad \underline{piano}$$
$$1 \qquad 1 \qquad 1$$

"I, have, brown," each total 9, so we have:

$$\underline{I} \quad \underline{have} \quad \underline{a} \quad \underline{lovely} \quad \underline{brown} \quad \underline{piano.}$$
$$9 \qquad 9 \qquad 1 \qquad 1 \qquad 9 \qquad 1$$

Some weeks passed, but the lady's faith did not waver. There was the promise, and it must be kept. While shopping one day she stopped before a display window. Within were several beautiful pianos, one of brown wood that particularly caught her fancy. "That's my piano," she thought. "I *have* a lovely brown piano," she insisted. At that moment a well-dressed woman came out of the shop. Her eyes met the eager glance of the window-shopper, and she smiled. Encouraged, the little woman called her attention to the particular instrument she liked. "Isn't that brown one a beauty," she exclaimed. "Why, yes, it is," the smiling stranger agreed. "It's almost a duplicate of my piano. I've just been inquiring about storage rates. I'm renting my home, furnished, but the tenants don't want to be responsible for the piano. They have a couple of vigorous little boys."

Almost breathlessly the little woman offered to store the instrument. It should have the best of care; she was a musician, and could give it exactly the use it should have to keep it from deteriorating.

The owner hesitated, then asked the address. This was furnished, also some good references, and after a further smiling assurance that the offer would be considered, the two women parted. But the heart of the one sang jubilantly: "I have a lovely brown piano. I have a lovely brown piano. I have a lovely brown piano."

Within a few days the stranger called, with her husband, saw the home into which her own beautiful instrument would go, and the

[134]

next day draymen were moving the piano into the space that had long been made ready for it.

Someone might ask: "Well, why couldn't she have met that stranger the day after she made her mantra?" Or, "Why did she have to wait several weeks?"

It has been the writer's experience that very often certain other conditions must first be met. In this instance it was the owner's removal from the city. "According to your faith be it unto you." Even though the manifestation was delayed, my patient's faith did not waiver. She had spoken the "word," had created the picture "above," and manifestation "below" was bound to follow. "As above, so below."

The sequel to this little story is, that the owner did not return to that city. She sold all her furniture. Although they had prospered, they considered the transportation of their piano too costly. It was then offered to my patient at a very low price, and she at last came into legal possession as well as spiritual ownership of the piano. In telling her story she said: "Of course, I felt that the piano actually belonged to me all the time. And the best part of it was, that the owner was happy in the knowledge that it was being cared for. When she did offer it for sale, she was satisfied that it would be used by one who really appreciated it, and who had treasured it as she herself had done."

At this point the writer wishes to again emphasize: The mantra must never be used to work injury to another. Happiness cannot be secured through the heart-ache of another. Only sorrow and defeat follow if the law is used to the detriment of one's fellows. Problems can always be solved constructively, with satisfaction to everyone concerned, and with injury to none. Therefore, it behooves each of us to so word our mantras that they accomplish the desired result without peril to ourselves or injury to another.

[135]

Again the reader is warned not to desire that which belongs to another. Put your desire in this way: There is a buyer for this land; one who can use it; one who desires it. Word your mantra accordingly. You want your buyer to be happy. You want whatever is *rightfully* yours. The right home that is for you and for no one else; the right conditions in your home; in your office; at your work bench. If you have a disagreeable foreman, work for freedom from his dominance. If it is inharmony in your home, your office, then work for peace. Are you seeking employment? Ask for the right opportunity. Picture yourself in the surroundings you desire.

All of this work must be done in a spirit of love. Remember that love is the most powerful force in the world. You bind yourself to unhappy conditions by hating them. Do not hate any one, or any condition. Free them with your mantras and let them go!

Appendix

In order that the reader may understand the movements of our earth and of the universe, as they were taught by the School of the Magi centuries ago, as is evidenced by the Great Pyramid of Gizeh. a definition of the astronomical terms used to explain these move-ments seems necessary.

Elliptic. A great circle in the heavens around which the sun seems to move. It completes a revolution every year. This movement seems to carry it from south to north across the equator and return, making the changes in our seasons. It is in reality the earth that moves, but the sun seems to do so. This *seeming* of things to our physical senses in contrast with the facts must ever be borne in mind. It constitutes the border line between the two worlds—the physical and the astral. What actually takes place is this: Both the sun and earth have an imaginary line through the center called the axis. In the annual revolution of the earth around the sun these lines are parallel on March 21 and September 21. At these times our days and nights are equal. On June 21 and December 21 the axis of the earth is inclined to that of the sun at an angle of 23.38 degrees. These are called the solistical points. They differ in this respect: On June 21 the north end of the earth's axis is inclined toward the sun. Then we have the longest days on the northern hemisphere. On December 21 the south end of its axis is inclined toward the sun. Then we have the shortest days on the southern hemisphere. Our senses acquaint us only with these changes in our seasons, not with the cause of them.

Celestial Equator. An imaginary circle in the heavens, the plane of which is always perpendicular to the axis of the earth. To illus-trate: If a horizontal line is drawn, and from the exact center of it another perpendicular line to it is also drawn, the top end of the second line will always point to the celestial equator. From the description given above of the periodic changes of the relation of

[137]

the axis of the earth to the axis of the sun, it will be understood that the top of our perpendicular line will, on March 21 and September 21, point directly at the sun; while on December 21 it will point north of it, and on June 21 will point south of it. Thus it will be seen that the sun is on the celestial equator twice each year. These are called the equinoxes. But our senses do not acquaint us with the cause of them.

Pole Star. This is a star at or near that point in the northern sky where the axis of the earth would, if extended, meet the heavens. Although the earth, in its annual revolution around the sun, describes a circle 180,000,000 miles in diameter, yet the distance between this star and the earth is so great that the north pole points in the direction of this star from every position in its circuit. The present pole star is called Polaris, and is in the constellation of Lesser Bear. It may easily be located by anyone on a clear night by following the direction of the "pointers," the two stars that form the wall of the Dipper opposite the handle.

Since the distance of these stars is so immense, when computed in miles, as to confound the imagination, astronomers resort to the speed of light to supply a convenient unit for the expression of these stellar distances.

Light travels approximately 186,000 miles per second. It requires forty-eight years for light to travel from Polaris to the earth. But our five senses tell us nothing of the immensity of space. Neither do they acquaint us with the speed at which our earth travels as it revolves upon its axis, producing the phenomena of day and night; nor of its rapidity as it travels around the sun, by which changes of our seasons are made. The former movement is over one thousand miles per hour, and the latter more than 1,500,000 miles per day.

Our universe, of which the sun is the center, with its seven or more planets similar to the earth, is making a revolution around a central sun or point, supposed by astronomers to be the Great Star

Alcyone, which is the brightest of the seven stars of the Pleiades in the constellation Taurus.

This vast journey of the earth, with its sun and sister planets, necessarily carries it away from one pole star and causes it, during the revolution to select others. These new selections are recorded by what is known as the precision of the equinoxes, a slow change of the point of intersection of the eliptic (apparent path of the sun) with the celestial equator. This causes the sun seemingly to move *backward* toward the west at the rate of fifty and three-quarters seconds each year. This backward movement of the equinoctial points causes the north pole of the earth to describe a circle in the heavens known as the "pole-star circle" around which the axis of the earth, if extended into the northern sky, travels every 25,800 years. By a simple computation that any astronomer can make, it can be known what stars have been or will be, at a given time, the pole star.

In this way it is known that when the great pyramid of Gizeh was built, the pole star was Alpha Draconis, the brightest star of the constellation Draco, or Great Serpent.

It is also known by the same means that had the pyramid been finished, its capstone, as a finger, would have pointed to Alcyone, the center of the Pleiades.

From this explanation, with which any astronomer will agree, we learn first: Our physical senses do not tell us the *truth* about the movements of our own earth, nor of its relation to the sun, moon, and other planets, of our universe. Second, that they can tell us *nothing* of the great clocklike movements of the universe as a whole, with other universes around the star Alcyone, which is the sun of our great universe.

Furthermore, these same physical senses deceive us as to what we call time. They tell us that yesterday is gone forever; that to-morrow is a future day; that last year will never again return. This great clock, whose hands revolve *backward* toward the *west,* instead of to the east, tells us plainer than words can tell, that we are moving toward bygone ages, that yesterday will come again, that tomorrow is in the past, and that next year was counted when the clock struck its number 25,800 years ago.

By means of calculation, as noted above, we know that the Great Pyramid of Gizeh was not built during the *last* time Alpha Draconis was the pole star. This was 2170 years B.C. We have history dating beyond this, as we reckon time here, which proves that the scientific knowledge of that period was not sufficient to qualify man to do such work. For these reasons, this great monument to intellectual man, could not have been built later than 25,800 years prior to that time. Its own chronology proves that it was built 53,770 years B. C.

Since this cyclopean structure testifies that there were highly developed men on earth long before the big clock started on its last revolution around the central star of its massive machinery 2170 B.C., we are justified as a race, in looking forward, or better, *backward,* to a time when that which has been will be again. The writer has endeavored to make it plain to the reader that our five physical senses, while useful in the care of the body, do not tell us anything concerning the great limitless universe in which we live, but actually deceive us concerning it.

It was through the ancient science of astrology that the Masters became acquainted with the movements of the heavenly bodies we call stars. The Greek word for *star* is aster, whence the mathematical science of the movements of the stars was called astrology. The region where these movements take place and the cause of them is called the astral world. The *region* is unlimited space. The *cause* is the great Universal Consciousness. "In Him we live, and move, and have our being."

Printed in the USA
CPSIA information can be obtained
at www.ICGtesting.com
LVHW081631281024
795040LV00039B/673

9 781564 595713